KU-015-088

Honda CBR900RR
FireBlade

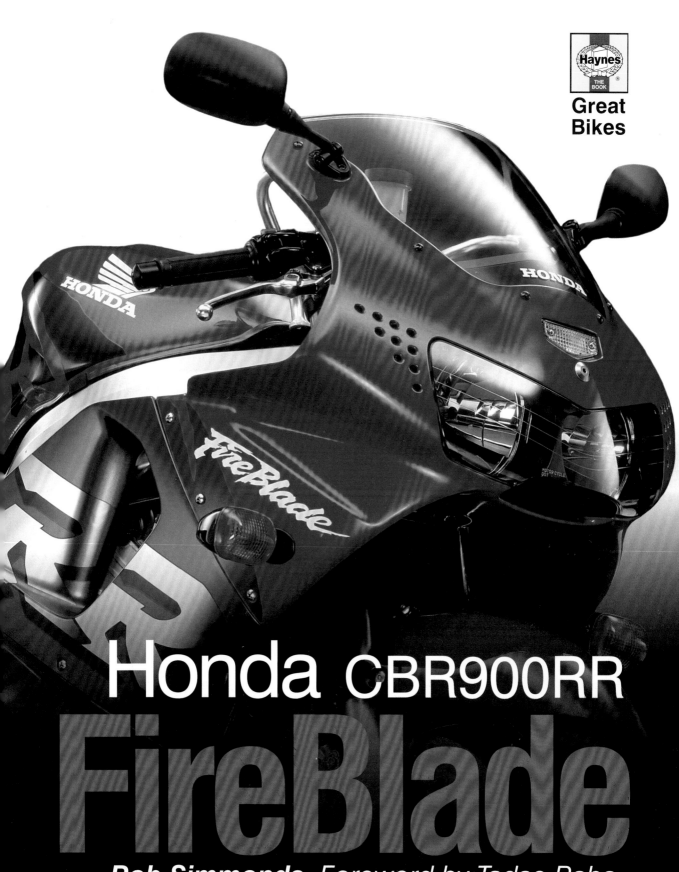

Haynes
THE BOOK
Great
Bikes

Honda CBR900RR
FireBlade

Rob Simmonds *Foreword by Tadao Baba*

MORAY COUNCIL LIBRARIES & INFO.SERVICES	
2O 12 47 1O	
Askews	
629.2275	

© Rob Simmonds 2000

All rights reserved. No part of this book may be reproduced in any form or by any means, electronic or mechanical, including photocopying, recording or by any information storage or retrieval system, without permission in writing from the copyright holder.

First published November 2000

A catalogue record for this book is available from the British Library

Published by Haynes Publishing,
Sparkford, Nr Yeovil, Somerset BA22 7JJ

Tel: 01963 442030 Fax: 01963 440001
Int. tel: +44 1963 442030 Fax: +1963 440001

E-mail: sales@haynes-manuals.co.uk
Web site: www.haynes.co.uk

ISBN 1 85960 640 7

Library of Congress catalog card no. 00-134247

Haynes North America, Inc.
861 Lawrence Drive, Newbury Park, California 91320, USA

Printed and bound in England by J. H. Haynes & Co. Ltd

Contents

Acknowledgements

Thanks to all of the following:

In the UK: *Bike* magazine, especially Paul Lang, Martin Child, Jenny Atyeo, Hugo Wilson, Richard Fincher, Steve Westlake, Dan Walsh, John Milbank, and Jeff Porter for the riding tips. *Performance Bikes*: Rob Gray, and especially Sally Barker and Trevor Franklin. *Motor Cycle News*: Sue Lynch, Pat Reynolds, Chris Moss, and Rob McDonnell. *Superbike* magazine: Warren Pole, John Cantilie and Dan Harris. Thanks also to: the MCRCB, British Superbikes 2000, Julian Ryder, and very special thanks to Phil McCallen.

At Honda UK: Dave Hancock, Steve Booth, Chris Herring, Dave Dew, and Scott Grimsdall. Thanks, too, to Honda Germany, Belgium, Austria, Australia, and France.

In Japan: the inspirational Tadao Baba of Honda R&D, without whom neither the FireBlade, nor many other cutting-edge bikes, would have been built. Also Satoshi Kogure of *Young Machine* magazine. And massive thanks to Yuko Sugeta.

In Greece: Vassilis Karachilous at *Moto Magazine*.

In Australia: *The Canberra Times*, and Ken Wootton at *Australian Motorcycle News*.

In South Africa: *Ride It* magazine.

In New Zealand: *Kiwi Rider* past and present, especially Jonathan Bentman; also *The Nelson Mail*, and *The North Otago & Regional News*.

In the United States: the good ol' boys at *Motor Cyclist*, including the late Greg McQuide (we miss you buddy) and Mitch Boehm; Dean Adams at *American RoadRacing* magazine; American Honda; and massive thanks to Kevin Erion of Erion Racing.

Picture acknowledgements
Many thanks to the following for all the beautiful images in this book:

Patrick Gosling and David Goldman at Gold and Goose; Double Red, especially James Wright; Roland Brown; Jason Critchell; Klicks Studio, Peterborough; Erion Racing and Ken Vreeke; Emap archives, especially Mandy Kirk at *Motor Cycle News*, and Ben Chantrell and Luke Brackenbury at *Bike* magazine; Jim Yeardly, Honda UK; and big thanks to Honda R&D in Japan for reproducing the original model illustrations at no cost whatsoever.

Also, thanks to all at Haynes for their patience, (and my other half), and my Uncle Kevin for getting me hooked on bikes in the first place!

Foreword

by Tadao Baba, CBR900RR FireBlade project leader

I remember being very pleased at the press launch of the Honda CBR900RR FireBlade.

I was pleased because the journalists were all so excited about this bike which the team and I had created – a bike which truly deserved the title 'super-sport'. But this feeling was surpassed when we saw sales of the FireBlade take off in the first year. That meant road riders were voting the bike *their* favourite by buying it in much larger numbers than we had dared hope.

Since then we have developed successive models to make it better and better, and to open up the FireBlade's performance to many new and different riders.

I love the CBR900RR FireBlade – I look upon it as one of my children, and hope that it lives on for ever – long after I'm gone. So for all of you FireBlade fans out there, here is its story.

Introduction

Short, squat, light, powerful and possessing an intimidating character, the Honda CBR900RR FireBlade was the seminal sportsbike of the 1990s.

From 1992 until almost the end of the decade, it ruled the road-bike roost, selling by the tens of thousands and introducing motorcyclists to a whole new level of performance previously seen only on racing machines. For the first time in decades, the CBR900RR FireBlade was a bike for which the development owed nothing to the marketing men in the giant Japanese motorcycle industry, but instead its existence was due to one, great man - Tadao Baba.

Baba-san was a visionary. He ignored the late 1980s trend for faster, heavier machines and, instead, concentrated on purifying the sportsbike by making it leaner, quicker turning and considerably meaner than ever before. In doing so he produced a machine that effectively made every other sportsbike obsolete.

Launched in the spring of 1992, the FireBlade made an instant impact, thanks to its combination of light weight and high power. In the UK and abroad, it became a popular machine, scooping numerous international awards and becoming a byword for sportsbike performance. Despite being the wrong capacity for most racing classes, the FireBlade even scored on the track, most notably at the Isle of Man TT races and in other forms of production-based racing.

In effect, the FireBlade changed the way sportsbikes were designed for ever, setting the trend for the latest crop of superbikes such as the Yamaha YZF-R1 and Kawasaki ZX-9R. Today, the latest generation of the CBR900RR FireBlade is still at the cutting-edge of sportsbike design, still selling in thousands and still giving motorcyclists everywhere the ride of their lives.

Want to make a FireBlade look tiny? Then simply put the author on board! *Bike* magazine's first UK track test for the Y2K CBR, Castle Combe, January 2000. (Jason Critchell)

Pure malevolence in aluminium. When shots of the CBR900RR FireBlade first leaked out to the press many were shocked by its squat, bullish looks. Could this really be a Honda? (Honda UK)

The origin of the species

The finest Japanese swordsmiths have known for more than a millennium that although a sharp blade can cut through steel and silk, it may nevertheless have a weakness that might cause it to break, or it might prove difficult to use. So, the smiths would sharpen and hone the edge of a sword to suit the particular person who would wield it and in accordance with the specific part of the blade that he would actually use.

Suzuka race circuit, 1989. The morning silence is broken intermittently by a high-pitched shriek, which indicates that a bike is being mercilessly thrashed around this legendary track.

Apart from the bike hardly a sound can be heard. There's no full grid of race machines to make a noise and no big crowd to roar them on. Security is tight. No cameras, nothing. Just a weird-looking, ugly bike and a handful of interested overall-wearing observers.

Every so often the grotesque machine pulls into the pits and stops in a garage. Almost

Tadao Baba: 'We wanted to build a bike that deserved the name "super-sport". (Yuko Sugeta)

immediately the rider is swamped by the observers. They are technicians, and on their backs they wear the 'flying wing' motif of the mighty Honda corporation. They interrogate the rider about engine performance, handling, and braking. Everything is noted down – engine position, suspension set-up. Then the rider is asked how the motor felt, what were the tyres like? Any scary moments? Did the seat feel comfy? Everything. And then some. High on adrenaline, the test rider answers the questions as best he can.

Changes are made, and the bike accelerates out of the pit-lane and back on to the track. The sound of the motor tells you it's a four-stroke, four-cylinder machine of 700–900cc or so capacity, but the crude sand-cast metal parts,

movable engine mounts, strange tank shape, fairing and chassis parts of indeterminable origin and overall shoddy finish do not tell you that this machine is an early pre-production version of a bike that will become a new byword for street motorcycle performance.

That bike burning up the track is an early ancestor of the Honda CBR900RR FireBlade, and in the next decade it will become the machine by which all other sportsbikes are to be measured.

One of the technicians isn't wearing any overalls; he's in leathers. He is Tadao Baba, chief engineer for Honda Research and Development. This is his first bike as project leader and the scuffs on his leathers tell you that he takes his work very seriously indeed.

Honda's previous big-bore mass-market sportsbike, the
CBR1000F, evolved into a capable sports tourer.
(Jason Critchell)

Fast forward ten years, and Baba-san remembers the original idea behind the bike. 'The CBR900RR made its debut in 1992, but it took us more than three years to reach that point. At that time the Japanese market was full of race-replicas, such as NSR250 and CBR400RR, while in Europe the power war had started with Kawasaki ZX10, GSX-R1100, and our CBR1000F. Up until then we called these bikes "Super-Sports", but we thought "wait a minute, are these big and heavy bikes really 'super-sports'?"

'We thought, going down a straight at high speed doesn't mean "super-sports". As it's a sportsbike, it must be *sporty*. The performance must be fun, easy and quick to control. A sport bike should be controlled freely as the rider

wishes. In this respect, all those big monsters were not good enough to be called sportsbikes. Yes, they were fast, but heavy and dull. We realised that we should create a completely new, enjoyable world for sportsbike lovers. We knew we must go back to the beginning, and start again. We wanted to give riders something over which they had total control.'

Initially the CBR1000F had been marketed as a 'super-sports' bike, but since its release in 1987 it had transformed itself from a cutting-edge sports machine into a more laid back sports tourer.

Baba-san: 'As the CBR1000's development proceeded, we had to think of practical aspects, such as driving long distance on an autobahn comfortably, taking a passenger on the pillion seat, and so on. Then, it became more like a tour bike. We wanted to keep it a bike that people could use on twisty roads and sweeping corners, but its ever-increasing weight made it impossible! From those ideals was born the CBR900RR FireBlade concept.'

Unusually, then, the impetus for the FireBlade project came from R&D, rather than the marketing men who were constantly looking for new opportunities and niche markets to exploit. At this very early stage the leader of the project was Oguma-san from Honda's racing division, Honda Racing Company (HRC). That alone shows that the image behind the bike was going to be that of a cutting-edge, no compromises sports machine.

After six months Oguma-san returned to HRC and the reins of responsibility were handed over to Baba. 'At this time,' recalls Baba-san, 'not even an egg of the 'Blade had been laid! We had only a very rough idea of what we wanted and very little design had been done, so the first step was to refine the idea and decide the machine layout. It was a very exciting appointment for me at the time. I knew the project would become very important for Honda, so I was highly motivated to make this machine a complete success.'

But with this being Baba's first time as a project leader – previously he'd been in charge of the R&D test team – he was understandably a little jittery.

'Of course I was nervous! But I was pretty confident, too, as I knew my strong points and weak points from my experiences at Honda up until then. I love riding an out-and-out sportsbike, and I love the feeling of satisfaction when I can control it as I want to. I knew my strong lust for conquest would lead the project in the right direction.'

For Baba-san this was the beginning of arguments, stress, and sleepless nights as he strove to make a bike with plenty of power and light weight.

He explains: 'I was happy to get this project – very happy. But the development life of the CBR900 was not always so cheerful. I suffered a lot. We all suffered a lot! Many times we got very stressed out and often we worked long hours through the night.'

Obviously, Baba's inexperience in leading a whole project team may have led to a number of clashes with other engineers, but he felt he knew what he wanted from each individual in the team and the contributions they could make to the final product.

'Most of the engineers were younger than I was,' he remembers, 'but they all had different backgrounds, and were specialists on chassis, engines, suspension, or whatever. I respected their thoughts and ideas and always listened to them. I understood that my work was to gather their best ideas and to bring them together as a whole product. A good engine doesn't sell a

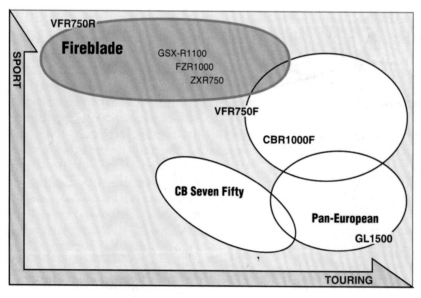

This shows just where Honda were pitching the CBR900RR project in its range. The FireBlade was to be sportier than the opposition and second only to its racer-for-the-road, the VFR750R RC30. (Honda UK)

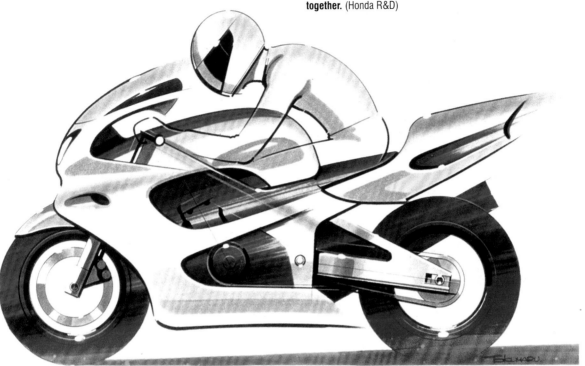

This early development sketch of the CBR900 shows that even at this stage the looks of the FireBlade were coming together. (Honda R&D)

bike. Nor does a good chassis. You have to bring these great ideas together and get them to gel – that's the secret.'

Professional conflict with other members of the team cropped up from time to time, as, understandably, long nights and a high stress environment took its toll.

'There were rumours that the young engineers would complain that when it came to cutting the weight of a component, "Baba-san never says yes". Apparently the young engineers used to call me "Hotoke no Baba", or "Buddha Baba" in English, maybe because I always thought I was right,' he laughs. 'Despite that I could be like a thunderstorm when I got angry. Maybe some of them were afraid of me; maybe they still are? It's because I can never let myself compromise – and we couldn't compromise on the weight of the CBR. I guess I'm pretty stubborn! I think age has made me milder, but others may not agree.'

Also, after years in a test position where he could tell engineers what was good or bad about their product, Baba now found that the

boot was on the other foot and he had to listen to what the test team said about his machine. 'Before, as a tester, I used to shout at the engineers when they made me ride a dangerous test bike. "How could you let me ride such trash?", I would say. But, suddenly, there was no more shouting.'

At the time the full specifications for the machine that would become the FireBlade were still not pinned down. In fact, it could well have become the CBR750RR, rather than a 900. At one stage a 750 version was tested by the triumvirate of European test riders, a fact which the ever-secretive Japanese later denied! Also, the prospects of an 1,100cc or 1,000cc power plant were dismissed when the merits of building a machine with a 'compromise' motor displacing around 900cc were discovered. Whatever motor would power the 'Blade, Baba-san was sure of one thing he wanted – as little weight as possible.

'That was our main aim,' recalls Baba. 'First of all, we wanted a big sportsbike which was actually lighter than a 600cc model. Then, to

Baba-san father of the FireBlade

A brief chat with Tadao Baba – executive chief engineer of Honda Research and Development – is enough to convince you he's motorcycle mad. Baba-san was born in 1944. He joined Honda in 1962 after graduating from high school at 18. A brush with the law proved to be his inauspicious debut into the heady world of motorcycles.

'A relative of mine had a Honda bike, but he never let me ride the thing,' he recalls. 'So, to satisfy my craving, I took a Super Cub from my father's garage, rode it without a licence, and got caught by police!'

Bitten by the bug, he saw one way of indulging himself in his passion while simultaneously carving himself out a fledgling career. He says: 'I only wanted to race bikes, so I thought I would be able to race as much as I wanted if I worked at Honda. That was my only motivation for joining. I believed I would make a top racer, even though I had never ridden a proper motorcycle at the time.'

He soon had a chance to indulge his passion.

'I started working at Honda factory in Saitama and joined their racing team. At the time the Saitama factory had some production CR racers and I was given an old model by a senior team mate. CR100, CR93, and CR77 were the bikes we were building then. It was about then that I also did a little motocross.'

At the time Baba-san had no real desire to get into bike design full time. He explains: 'I was young, so was only thinking of my next race. I raced until I was 25, and even since quitting I have been to our test track every week to test all the bikes from Honda. I still do it now. I can't stop myself!'

Eventually he worked his way into the major design teams responsible for some very important machines.

'The first CB750F was my milestone,' he recalls. 'I tested the bike from the start. I was pretty outrageous at that time. When I was there, there was always somebody crashing, as apparently my demands during testing made the test riders mad! I really enjoyed the test, though. In 1970, I went to America for the first time, for a month, to test the bike. It was a great experience. Then I was in the project team for CB350F, and then 400F.'

What followed were spells spent on the test teams of various Honda trial and trail bikes, before a five-year stint on the emission measurement team. Then a move to work as a carburation engineer took him further away from riding test bikes. 'When I was first offered the job I refused,' he says. 'I wanted to keep riding, not to stay in a room to study a tiny hole in the carb. Then my boss told me off. He said to control bikes better, I must study carbs. I was young and he was right.'

At the time there was none of the specialisation you see today in R&D departments.

'Now our jobs are very specialised, carb engineers just do carbs, chassis designers do chassis. But we used to do everything. For the racing as well. I'm sure this helped my career a lot.'

Bikes still dominate Baba-san's life – even more so

gain the right stability for the machine, the chassis dimensions and riding position were fixed during our extensive testing. So at the end of all this we find that there is a limited space for the engine. With the space we had left we thought we could go for something bigger than 750cc. We really wanted a motor that could push this bike to around 161mph [260kph] – that would be enough. From this data we could find exactly what maximum power we would need for the bike to get to this speed and from there what the displacement of the motor would have to be. That turned out to be 893cc. Obviously in later years we would up the displacement to more than 900cc. Like the drop in weight, we also found we could squeeze more from the power plant. But at the beginning we chose the layout of the best machine from a number of different options. These were not so different, as the direction was the same and the ideal was the same: optimum power with as little weight as possible. We had to decide where to draw the line, where we stopped scrutinising each individual part. It was a big hurdle to get over at first, but with subsequent models we've managed to mature the product little by little.'

with the work on the latest evolution of the FireBlade.

'I get to go to karaoke occasionally,' he says, 'but my life is devoted to motorcycles. I used to play soccer (I was a striker), but since I joined Honda my life has been motorcycles and motorcycle racing. I still go to the test track every week, even as executive chief engineer. Of course, young test riders are faster than me, but I have more experience than they do. I understand what is wrong and what is right more clearly and quickly than they do. Maybe these young people say "Oh God, here he comes again! Can't he trust us and leave us alone?"

'When I find something wrong, I come back to the pits immediately after a lap, and tell them. When I don't come back to the pit immediately, that's when I love the bike very much or I feel something wrong but don't know what it is. That's why, while they're waiting for me, young test riders seem to be biting their nails! But I can't be responsible for the bikes we make without riding them. Call me a company man, but I don't regret it, as I still love motorcycling. I also love reading books about Japanese history. Since my son has grown up and left home, I'd like to do something nice for my wife – like go on a trip together – but, I don't have much time.'

So what does the future hold for out-and-out sportsbikes like the FireBlade?

'As human beings we love competition,' he says, 'and as long as we have our fighting instinct, sportsbikes like the FireBlade will never die.'

Company man: Tadao Baba outside Honda R&D, Japan.
(Yuko Sugeta)

The Europeans help out

It was early in the test schedule in 1989 when Dave Hancock from Honda UK became involved in the project. He was one of three test riders, (the others being Bernard Rigoni from Honda France and Klaus Bescher from Honda Germany) who, throughout the test programme, would test Honda's latest creations in their varying forms for their suitability to the European market. Honda USA and Japan had their own testers, mainly for the reason that many models for those parts of the world were pretty much exclusive to their own markets, such as the 400 four-stroke class in Japan and the big cruiser market in the USA.

'I still remember the first time I rode the bike at Suzuka in 1989,' recalls Dave. 'We had two days with this new bike. At the time they had decided on the 900cc displacement. (I'd ridden the 750 version earlier, even though the Japanese later denied categorically that they actually had such a machine!) Also at this time it was fitted with a 17-inch front wheel as

This early production model of the first FireBlade shows 'mass centralisation' at work. Big, heavy parts like the engine are all positioned in the middle of the bike. (Honda UK)

opposed to the 16 which the machine would later use. It wasn't the prettiest thing on two wheels, but then again not many test bikes were. The chassis was a bit of a mish-mash of movable engine mounts, sand-cast bits and pieces, and a swingarm that, I think, came from a CBR1000. The tank also was nothing that you could really recognise. The engineers would experiment with different shapes and sizes in a bid to get something with the right shape for

your legs and the right amount of fuel and the correct weight distribution. You'd come into the pits and the engineers would want to know everything. How the motor felt, suspension, the lot. Even if the bike didn't look like much – and sometimes these pre-production development machines really looked pretty disturbing – it was surprising just how good even these early machines felt.'

Certain motorcycling fashions of the time

over in Europe led to the testers wanting small changes made to the design of the bike, even at this early stage.

Hancock: 'We all told Baba-san that the bike really needed upside-down [inverted] front forks. At the time the fashion was for upside-downers, as most race machines were using them, but Baba was insistent. "They weigh too much," he would tell us. He was always emphasising the problems of having too much weight or having mass and weight in completely the wrong place. That's part of the reason why the bike had no rear hugger covering the back wheel, as the CBR600 has, and they made sure it didn't need a steering damper on the road because that would simply add too much weight.'

At every stage Baba and the development team wanted to weigh up whether a part really needed to be on the bike. For the FireBlade development team, the best parts of a bike were the ones you could do without, hence keeping the weight down.

Early on in the design process Baba and his team decided to go against the then current thinking and utilise a 16-inch rather than a 17-inch front wheel.

'We tested both the 17-inch front wheel and a 16-inch front wheel during the entire test process,' reveals Hancock, 'but eventually, after a lot of work, Baba and the team made the decision to go with the 16-inch front with all the weight-saving advantages that came with it.'

After two gruelling days at Suzuka the test circus headed to Honda's Tochigi proving ground, which is just over an hour from Tokyo.

'Tochigi has pretty much every type of corner and surface so you can really test a bike,' says Hancock. 'Really, this is when the bike starts to be given a thorough testing in the sort of conditions that the finished machine will be used in on the road. Nearly every powered machine that Honda produces can be tested there. Cars, road and off-road bikes, and even ATVs [all terrain vehicles], the whole lot. The level of grip on the circuits is simply fantastic. You've got everything from a 45-degree banked, high speed circuit through to a cobbled road and a twisty handling circuit. There's every conceivable corner at Tochigi,

and they even lay on coaches so you can get to all the different sections of the complex. It's not unusual to sometimes see cars and bikes being tested at the same time on the same track.'

Testing high-performance motorcycles at such a dedicated test track is not without its dangers – or surprises – as Hancock found out:

'On the high-speed banking there's a white line which indicates that you're one metre away from the Armco at the top part of the banking. I found it hard to get used to swinging up high on the banking; it's a weird feeling, but some of the top Japanese boys could go over the white line. On more than one occasion I found myself flat-out on the FireBlade, shaving the white line with my front wheel, with one of the other testers overtaking me with his elbows brushing the Armco. Amazing stuff. I love going to Tochigi. It's like a fairground for someone into bikes and cars – and all the rides are free! The best thing is that you're safe in the knowledge that no-one is going to pull out on you.'

All three European testers obviously had different opinions and each was chosen for a different reason. 'We may ride at different speeds and we are different shapes and sizes,' says Hancock, 'but all this helps the Japanese to refine the bike to suit a wide range of people. If any one of us was not happy with a particular element of the machine's development then the process would not move on until the tester was happy. That's vitally important, because in general, Honda do not want to make any mistakes that could prove to be costly – and they certainly didn't with the 'Blade. If a problem arises, then we iron it out and put the bike through a re-test. Only if we are all happy can the design progress to the next stage.'

From Tochigi the bikes may be tested away from Japan, mainly in Europe – unless it's a Continent-specific machine, like a cruiser for the American market.

Hancock: 'We did a fair amount of autobahn testing with the 'Blade in Germany, testing the bike at speed on "proper" roads. That's when the size difference between me and Klaus Bescher was apparent. Because I'm so small and light I had a problem with the bike in windy conditions – I was getting buffeted about quite a bit. But Klaus, who's a fair bit heavier, didn't have such problems. That's when it's important to have testers of all shapes and sizes. Sometimes it was a hard job to convince the Japanese what the problems you were experiencing were, but once they knew, they did their best to eliminate them.'

Two years after that first test in Suzuka, Baba-san and the project team moved to the challenging Circuit Van Drenthe near Assen in northern Holland, renowned as a tough riders' circuit with fast, flowing banked corners. This is where the test team recruited a new member – someone who had great experience with race and road bikes.

Hancock: 'I remember telling Baba-san and the engineering team that we must get someone who can really ride the FireBlade and really test this thing. That's why I thought of road-racer Phillip McCallen. We knew each other fairly well at the time. Honda like people who project the right image – professionalism is paramount. I was hoping that when he turned up at the circuit Phillip would fit the bill. Thankfully he'd obviously had a think about that too, and he turned up in immaculate white leathers with Honda logos on them. He really looked the part. Before he came along the testing for Honda R&D was a bit of a closed shop to anyone outside of Honda. To give Phil his due he got straight on that thing and rode the wheels off it – almost! And he gave the engineers lots of feedback. He gave them so much information about geometry set-up and the like that the engineers themselves had to remind him that this was a road bike, not a race machine.'

Phil McCallen has had a long association with the Honda FireBlade, reaching right up to the 1998-9 version, and he still remembers how he got involved with Honda R&D and his first encounter with the machine.

'Dave got me the testing job with Honda,' remembers McCallen. 'At the time, I heard through the grapevine that Honda were developing a real super-sports machine and I was pleased when I was asked to come to the Assen test of the bike in 1991. I guess I was chosen because I was pretty much knocking on the door of a win at the TT and they wanted someone who currently raced so they could see just how good this bike was.'

As soon as the Ulsterman got to the track he was in no doubt as to how important the bike was to Honda.

'It didn't take a scientist to work that out,' he recalls. 'The security at the Van Drenthe Circuit was particularly tight and the size of the presence from Honda R&D was astounding. They had two 40-foot trucks and trailers which carried every different part that the riders needed to test. They even brought one huge truck to bring test tyres alone!'

As this was McCallen's first test, it was good that Hancock was on hand to pass on some advice. McCallen explains: 'I remember Dave telling me that I had to be really consistent to be able to test a bike fully. You can't just string a couple of laps together and think that will do. Thanks to my experience of road and short circuit racing, I found I could set up the bike well and could ride it hard enough to give the Japanese technicians plenty of feedback on everything from chassis and suspension to carburation and tyres. I found I could tell them various things about the bike after only a couple of sessions and I think the Japanese were a little bit surprised by that. The bike had the 16-inch front wheel by then and that made it a little sensitive, but also made it turn that much quicker. It was a flexible arrangement because it meant lighter weight and the desirable turning characteristics of a 17-inch profile.'

Although this was the later stages of testing, many bugs and problems still had to be ironed out. Despite this, the feedback that the riders got from the bike made them all realise they were on something special.

McCallen recalls: 'Even at that time I knew that this was a bike with a lot of character. It really showed through when we tested the bike back-to-back with the latest machines of the time.'

In 1991 the current crop of cutting-edge sportsbikes were behemoths. Big, bloated, and brash, they pushed their way through the air with spiralling power curves and, almost yearly, creeping weight gains.

At the time the real sports competition

Dave Hancock Honda Europe test pilot

Dave Hancock (*MCN*)

'I was born in 1954 in Stoke-on-Trent, left school at 16, and wanted to get straight into bikes,' says Hancock. 'I didn't want to do anything else. I started road racing Yamahas pretty much as soon as I could. After I started racing I met TT star Charlie Williams and he began to slip me some old bits for my bike. I always kept my bikes immaculate – even if I wasn't doing too well at the time. I remember Charlie coming over to me when I was racing at Oulton Park, in Cheshire, and he said: "I've seen you ride, Dave, and I reckon you'll make a better mechanic than a racer", and that was that. I spannered Charlie's bikes for the next six years.'

Hancock later worked for Yamaha, organising the successful Pro-Am series in the early 1980s, in which the embryonic talents of Niall Mackenzie, Kenny Irons, and even Formula 1 car star Damon Hill first saw the light of day.

'Following that I went to work in a dealership as a salesman,' he recalls, 'but I was worse than terrible at it. But I still managed to become general manager of the store.' Pretty soon after that, Hancock was offered a job by Mervyn Smith, then boss of Honda UK.

'I couldn't refuse working for Honda. I've been with them about 12 years now. I've been national sales manager, sales and marketing manager, servicing manager – you name it, I've done it. In fact I think no other Honda employee in Europe has covered all the jobs in all the departments that I have.'

By the beginning of the 1990s, Hancock was also employed as a test and development rider for Honda Europe, on the say-so of current Honda UK boss Bob McMillan. 'I always have a set of leathers and a helmet at work,' says Hancock, 'because Honda R&D can call us in at a moment's notice, so all the test riders can pretty well be in Japan and testing within about 24 hours.'

Despite more than a decade of sterling service, only now has he been allowed to see inside the hallowed portals of Honda's R&D facility. Hancock explains: 'It was Osaka's R&D section, and I was like a kid in a sweet shop. They still didn't trust me completely, as some of the stuff in there was covered up.'

Such a seal of approval indicates in just what high esteem Hancock is held – but it goes both ways. 'I've had to make Honda my life,' he says, 'and I don't regret that. Their reputation is second to none. To illustrate: I had a phone conversation once with a guy who'd got a 1972 CB750. It had done 35,000 miles in its long life and he'd rung up to complain that it had started to leak a little oil! I explained to him that after all this time that's pretty good going, but he said: "I bought a Honda for its reliability, it shouldn't leak oil!" That tells you what a reputation for quality we have and what sort of standards our customers are used to. I'm proud to be part of that.'

consisted of the Suzuki GSX-R1100, which possessed massive power and an antiquated frame design that saw most of its bulk positioned high up – not conducive to ease of handling; the ZZ-R1100 from Kawasaki, which boasted probably the best motor of the time, although it was more of a sports tourer compared to the Suzuki; and the Yamaha FZR1000EXUP.

The EXUP was widely recognised as the best sportsbike of the time. It had a slanted forward 1,000cc 20-valve motor which used the Yamaha-patented power-boosting EXUP valve, wrapped in a Deltabox aluminium beam frame, upside-down front forks, and an aero-dynamically slippery fairing.

This was the main contender that the new machine had to beat.

'At that test we had a GSX-R1100, Yamaha's EXUP, Honda's own CBR1000F, and a ZZ-R1100 to test against the FireBlade,' says McCallen. 'Again, with such back-to-back testing consistency was the key. To fully compare the machines you couldn't have a bad session on one particular bike, otherwise you wouldn't be giving the Japanese technicians the comparative feedback they needed to refine the 'Blade. It was tough, but rewarding. As a racer, I found during the sessions that I was the fastest tester on all the bikes, so that meant they would definitely be listening to what I had to say.'

In fact, both McCallen and Baba-san himself would get more than a little carried away during testing.

'I got so caught up in what I was doing and so carried away with the bike that I ground away the foot-peg and started to grind the exhaust away,' recalls McCallen. 'I said to the engineers, "do you want me to go any faster?" They shouted at me, "no more, please McCallen-san!" To give you an indication of just how hard the test schedule was, I remember

Baba-san himself crashing the FZR when chasing the times set by the FireBlade.'

After just a few sessions it was easy to see that the new Honda model had more than the measure of its rivals.

McCallen: 'Pretty much all the testers could go between 1.9 and 2 seconds quicker on the FireBlade than the other machines – that made it a winner straight away. Then the object was to try to beat the FireBlade times on the other bikes.'

This proved more difficult. The testers found that although some of the other bikes felt faster, more than often they weren't.

McCallen explains: 'The speed of the CBR was so deceptive. You'd get off the other bikes and be sure you'd beaten your time on the FireBlade, but you'd rush to the timekeeper and find you were still two seconds shy of your time on the 'Blade. We finally put it down to the almost "lazy" feel of the Honda. You could feel a real discernible powerband on the other bikes but not so on the CBR; it was almost like a twin in some ways. I guess that's what made the bike so good, it had good torque and seemed easier than the others to ride fast. With the Yamaha, the power came in like a missile, but comparatively you needed a lot of effort to turn it into corners.'

If one criticism could be levelled against the CBR during tests, it was that 'lazy' feel. Almost a lack of acceleration or a lack of involvement.

'We all felt that the motor wasn't as quick as the others,' says McCallen, 'and that's despite the lap times. To teach us a lesson the engineers changed a few things such as the cam timing and some other things in the CBR's motor to give us more of a powerband, and told us to tell them what we thought. After another session and loads more laps we came back telling them that it felt so much faster than before – but we found that the lap times and top speeds were actually down on the previous

Black is black: mean, moody and magnificent… the 1992 FireBlade.

development motor. That proved their theory on what the engine should feel like and we couldn't complain anymore. At the end of the two-day test most of the testers agreed that none of us had ridden a bike like the Honda CBR900RR FireBlade before; it was a revelation. I couldn't wait for the bike to come out the following year. I had to have one!'

If Hancock found the testing punishing, things would get more difficult for him as he got to know and appreciate the FireBlade's qualities.

'During the actual testing you have to really explain what any differences feel like to the

Japanese technicians,' he says. 'It can be long, tough, tiring work. But rewarding. The thing was, when I came back to the UK from these tests it was so hard not to tell anyone about the FireBlade. Here was a bike that I knew would blow the socks of anyone who rode it and knock spots off the competition, but I had to keep quiet. It was agony! All the testers have to sign a secrecy document and none of us has broken that vow, but it's still hard not to tell anyone. It's like when you have a cracking ride on your bike and you want to tell someone, anyone, about it. But harder! I remember telling Bob McMillan – boss of

Honda UK – about how hard it was to keep quiet at the time.'

Despite Hancock and co keeping tight-lipped, firstly the Japanese and then the world press got to hear about this amazing new machine.

Rumours trickled out. Was it to be a CBR750RR? Or maybe a 1000, or an 1100? Inverted front forks? V-four? Fuel-injection?

What was clear was that the new machine would be an uncompromising sports machine. Most of the rumours included talk of the 'RR' designation, which signified it as an out-and-out sports machine, as opposed to the 'F' range of machines, which indicated more of an all-rounder. Whatever it was, it would be a Honda, and many people thought that should mean something very special indeed.
But it had to be launched at the right time and have the right motor and the right name.

As well as looking at the engineering reasons why a 900cc motor could be the way to go, there were marketing reasons too.

Hancock recalls: 'Honda's previous "sports" flagship model, the CBR1000F, was still selling well as it was, so it was felt that we needed to develop a separate model to fire up the super-sports class. We tested a CBR750RR, which is what the FireBlade could have been, but it was thought that another 750 might affect sales of both the CBR600 and the VFR750 – which were both selling exceptionally well around the world. Eventually, that and engineering concerns, led us to the 893cc motor. It gave us another class category, in which we were in a class of one.

'My memory is still a little shaky on exactly who came up with the name,' recalls Hancock. 'We were all huddled around a table discussing various names for the CBR900RR and I think it was Laurent Chaveux from Honda France that may have actually come out with that very name – it's sort of an English translation of the Japanese word for "Lightning". It was an

inspired piece of genius, because the name is still a byword for performance. Instantly recognisable, even by non-bikers. You get a fair bit of respect from people when you tell them you've got a FireBlade.'

Towards the end of the development phase of the 'Blade, many people in Honda felt they were on to a winner, but the whole process was still not finished. Any bugs had to be ironed out.

'Towards the end of the design and development stage there's an initial production run where an initial quality check (IQC) is made,' says Hancock. 'We obviously ride the bike and give it a thorough testing to make sure everything is in order. Many of the parts for these machines are still not mass manufacture, but after the test we can make changes to the overall design of the machine, hand the altered blueprints to the guys at the beginning of the production line, and say "build us 20,000 of those…"

'Even after production has started we can react pretty quickly and make small changes on the line as the bikes are coming off at the other end. For example, we found on early examples of the '92 'Blade that the brakes started to bind, but we soon cured the problem.'

The biggest test of all, though, is when the bike finally goes on sale.

'That's when you can start to get butterflies,' admits Hancock, 'because no matter how thoroughly you test a bike it's the public who really test it after launch. You could theoretically still get things wrong, despite the fact that at Honda we do our best to minimise this.'

Almost four years after the initial development, at the end of 1991, finally, the bike was nearly ready to be unleashed on an (almost) unsuspecting public.

Neither the press, public, Honda R&D, or even Baba-san could really believe just how big this bike would be when it was finally launched at Phillip Island race circuit in Australia on a cloudy but dry day in February 1992.

Phillip McCallen Blade sharpener...

Phillip McCallen – like many racers before him – started out racing because he was sure he'd kill himself on the road. 'It was in 1984 when I realised I was just doing some bloody stupid things on the road,' he explains. Unfortunately he was still doing silly things on the road in cars, which is why he missed the 1985 season through injury. 'I was racing a mate in his Ford Fiesta XR2 when I hit a dry stone wall head on in a car at about 80mph [128kph].' The incident left him with a badly injured left leg.

He made his Isle of Man debut at the Manx GP in 1988, taking a record-breaking win in the Lightweight Newcomers and the regular Lightweight classes – the first and only time a rider has ever achieved this. The following year he made his first appearance at the TT and finished 15th in the Formula 1, seventh in the Ultra-Lightweight, and 17th in the Senior.

Phil finally turned pro-racer in 1990 and that year he staged an inspired comeback in the Junior race where he battled back from 39th place to a magnificent sixth. The result almost made up for the disappointment of crashing out of the Senior while holding a fine third place.

McCallen finished tantalisingly close to a win in 1991 with second in the Junior and third in the Senior. It was around this time that Honda began to get very interested in him. As he mastered road circuits such as the Isle of Man TT course, the North West 200, and the Ulster GP, he was seen as the natural successor to countryman Joey Dunlop as 'King of the Roads', and Honda, especially its UK arm, felt that success for Honda's products on 'real' road circuits was paramount to selling more and more road machines.

His first TT win came in 1992, riding a Castrol Honda RC30 in the Formula 1 race against Island greats Steve Hislop (on a Norton), Dunlop (on an RC30), and future World Superbike champion Carl Fogarty (on a Loctite Yamaha). He also scored his second win that year, in the Supersport 600 race.

McCallen is still the only man in history to have won four TT races in a week, when he scooped top honours in the F1, Senior, Production, and Junior TTs in 1996. His current TT win tally stands at 11. He later began mixing short circuit racing with his road races, running at the front of the British and European Thunderbike classes before the switch to Supersport 600 rules.

In May 1998 he broke his back in the Supersport 600 series at Thruxton, Hampshire, which saw him miss that year's TT races. Bad luck hit his plans for the 1999 TT as well, when he crashed at Donington

Every speeder's worst nightmare – Phillip McCallen on a police-spec FireBlade. (Double Red)

Park during the British Sports Production race while setting up his Yamaha YZF-R1 for the TT. Despite a torn shoulder blade and muscle he nevertheless finished third in the Production Race on a Yamaha YZF-R1 and seventh in the Junior race on a Yamaha YZF-R6.

The 'Portadown Flyer' is still not 100 per cent retired from racing, but he's now spending more and more of his time as a manager for Bristol-based Motorcycle City.

Tiddly 296mm rotors, fake upside-down forks and a small, 16-inch front wheel. Less is more as the bike scooped accolade after accolade. (Roland Brown)

Fear and loving –
reaction to the FireBlade

Honda had not done anything like it before. Its top performance model of the 1991 season was the CBR1000F, an accomplished machine, sure, but not one to really set your pulse racing. It had gone through years of development during which it had been transmogrified from a big bore sportsbike into a comfy supertourer. Honda, it was generally felt, was a manufacturer that built great bikes with a build quality to die for – but anything resembling character was sadly lacking.

Then in 1992 it happened. Honda released a machine with the weight of a 600 but with a motor shoehorned into a light aluminium chassis that had the power of a 1,000cc machine. To cap it all they gave it a cool name – the FireBlade. And then the men from the 'flying wing' displayed the most wonderful macabre arrogance by painting it black and gunmetal, almost as if to scare off potential buyers.

How could an attitude-ridden super sports machine like this fit into a range of machines which included the district nurses' favourite the C90, and the courier's virtueless NTV600? It just didn't make sense. But like other Hondas in other classes before it, the 'Blade simply rewrote the rules. At the time, super sportsbikes were generally in the 750cc bracket, while the 1,000–1,100cc class had the likes of Yamaha's superb EXUP, Suzuki's bloated GSX-R1100, and Kawasaki's sports-touring ZZ-R1100. Honda arrogantly – and quite correctly – decided not to conform to either. After all, it still had the limited edition RC30 to race in the 750 Superbike class, it had the supremely capable VFR750 to sell to the masses, and it had the CBR1000F to take on the big boys in the sports-touring class, and so, with the luxury of such a large range of machines in other categories, the FireBlade could carve a niche of its own. And carve it did.

The UK's Motor Cycle News first carried information and a picture of the new machine as early as February 1991 – a whole year before the launch. They managed to get hold of an official factory side-on shot of the CBR for an October 1991 issue. 'Squat and chunky, Honda's power-packed CBR900RR is to scorch the showroom floors in springtime,' they announced. 'Our picture shows that the FireBlade is the Olympic powerlifter among bikes. Never before has so much brute force been engineered into such compact dimensions.'

Australian Motorcycle News managed to beat the world's press to first glimpses of the 'Blade just prior to the launch. Squat and purposeful, many could not believe it was a 900! (*AMCN*)

Motorcycle press local to the launch at Phillip Island managed to get a sneak glimpse of the CBR900RR just prior to the official launch in February 1992. *Australian Motorcycle News* – that continent's leading bike magazine – took advantage of their biweekly lead times to bring their readers an exclusive first peek at the new superbike before the official embargo date. Riding shots and comments were forbidden, but it was still the first good look at the bike that anyone had had.

'You couldn't help but be impressed with it,' recalls *Aussie MCN* editor Ken Wootton, who was allowed to sit astride the machine and wheel it around for photos.

'It wasn't the flashy graphics, or the racy Swiss-cheese holes in the fairing, or the fat look-alike slick Bridgestone tyres that impressed, it was what's missing that did it – bulk, weight, and physical size. I remember saying at the time that everything the international hype had made the bike out to be looked spot on. Wheeling it around for pictures you almost forgot it was a 900.

'The bike has certainly captured the imagination of the motorcycling public,' said Wootton at the time, 'the FireBlade pushes the '90s thrust of "bigger is better". After all, when

In February 1992 this was every sportsbike fan's dream. A line of brooding CBRs each with a tank full of gas and a bellyful of fire. (Gold and Goose)

have you heard of an open-class sportsbike which claims *less* power than its opposition being so eagerly awaited?'

With a four-year development period it was obvious that morsels of information were going to get out. In the end the CBR900RR was one of the worst kept secrets of motorcycling. Even the official Honda importers in the USA leaked pictures of a test rider in action on the FireBlade to *Cycle World*.

With so much anticipation, pre-publicity, and hype, the bike needed to be very good indeed. For project leader Tadao Baba, it was an exciting time – but worrying too.

'In February 1992, when we held the world launch at Phillip Island, many journalists came to us after riding the FireBlade. They had had so much fun and gotten so excited they wanted to compliment us. I was thrilled. At the same time, I knew it didn't mean the bike would be successful in the marketplace, and obviously that was our main concern. But it was good to know they liked our product, and that meant the press response should be very positive indeed.'

Initial press reports from Phillip Island race circuit, near Melbourne, were astounding, but even seasoned hacks were wary of this beast

Sean Emmett – future GP rider and later British Superbike star – gets some airtime at Phillip Island in his role of road tester for the UK's *Fast Bikes* magazine. (Gold and Goose)

Aim at the horizon and hit the throttle. Many found the FireBlade a bit of a handful on Phillip Island's gorgeous curves, with some claiming that a steering damper was needed. (Gold and Goose)

that simply oozed malevolence just from the spec sheet.

Respected freelance journalist and ex-Isle of Man TT racer, Mac McDiarmid summed it up best when he wrote at the launch: 'The numbers that Honda bandied about were exciting: a 900 pumping out poke like a good 1,100, yet weighing in the same poundage as a pretty light 600. But as the hour of reckoning approached, other numbers began to prevail. Numbers like: trail 89mm (3.5in), wheelbase 1,405mm (55.3in); this was territory only seen on the small, perfectly formed sportsbikes like Kawasaki's KR-1S, the sort of figures that put a lightweight 250 on the twitching edge of stability. What that might do to a full-blown 900 shoving out 120-odd ponies had us worried. What they'd do to the same 900 with a 16-inch

front wheel had us scared.'

The 16-inch front wheel (most modern bikes of the time had 17-inchers) may have bestowed the bike with a flighty feeling for the uninitiated, but it also meant it could turn quicker than most riders could think. 'This thing,' explained McDiarmid, 'doesn't so much steer quickly as keep dematerialising and appearing somewhere else.'

Motor Cycle News's tester Chris Dabbs had worries of his own. 'I definitely didn't feel in control as I pushed the FireBlade through the first 10-minute test session at Phillip Island,' he recalls. 'Rain clouds were gathering and the journos were starting to label the bike a wobbler. "Steering damper" was a phrase that filled my brain as I came back into the pits. "No need for steering damper, we test flat-out on

autobahns," was the response from Baba-san the chief engineer. I'm not saying the bike's unstable, but a bit of extra security wouldn't have gone amiss as the front end was so light and quick.'

Aussie MCN's Wootton – who knew the launch track of Phillip Island better than anybody – could hardly believe the capabilities of the bike. And he also reckoned on the need for a steering damper.

'The CBR is quite twitchy at full stick,' he said. 'The short wheelbase and ample power gets the front end light, so much so that I had a tank-slapper leaving the pit lane when I really wasn't expecting the front to rear skywards. The same happened on the rumble strip on the start/finish straight. The bars slapped back and forth for 50 metres until the thing regained composure – and this was at 230kph [142mph]. There was a group of us who managed to dip into the 1m 51s bracket and we all agreed that on the street we'd put on a steering damper.'

He added: 'That's not to say the CBR is a bad handler – far from it. It's just that this bike is a precision instrument which rewards smooth input, and with ample power and such a light weight it gets a little flighty (and exciting) at full noise – have a look at the specs if you want proof. Try to imagine a production 250 bike with a big engine and you'll get my drift. Actually, it's more of a 500GP bike for the street…'

Forget what you hear about journalists selflessly testing motorcycles for the benefit of you, the buyer. Generally sportsbike launches end up with riders from the same group racing each other like demented madmen. Sometimes challenges are even issued in the pit lane prior to a wheel turning in anger. The FireBlade launch was no different – except this time the bike's capabilities generally exceeded those of most of the riders present.

Wootton did his best to keep Aussie pride intact. 'I streaked across the finish line, past the Honda technician holding the chequered flag and under the Dunlop bridge, my black European-spec CBR900RR heading the other two into the braking area. The 250m board was as far as I got with my nose in front. First it was

Sean Emmett from Fast Bikes magazine who pulled out of my slipstream and whistled by on my left, followed a micro-second later by MCN's Chris Dabbs. He blasted both of us on the right as he got the benefit of our two-bike "hole in the air" slipstream, shooting from third to first. I'd been pulling over 260kph [161mph] and my "mutha country" colleagues were catapulted to towards 270kph [168mph] as we all went for the anchors, clicked it down a cog and peeled into the very fast Turn One, for all intents and purposes three abreast. Bloody hell, this wasn't supposed to be a 500 race, or even a competitive thrash! We were all supposedly objectively testing the new FireBlade! "That was great fun," said Emmett to me afterwards. "Did you see the crowd watching us at Turn One?" No, we weren't supposed to be racing, but our little dice together underlines the confidence we'd all built up in the CBR900RR by the end of the day, and there was nothing wrong with having a little bit of fun before handing the keys back to the Honda Europe personnel.'

Superbike magazine's editor – the late John Cutts – was also impressed: 'Honda hope to sell 1,500 of these in the UK. I reckon they'll sell out. The FireBlade has enough performance to be called Honda's first real hooligan tool, but it wouldn't be a Honda without having consummate manners. Just as it was looking extremely unlikely, maybe the big sportsbike has a future after all.'

Riding the CBR900 on billiard-table smooth racetracks was one thing; testing out a twitchy missile like the 'Blade on bumpy, pot-holed British roads must surely be another. Especially as many had commented at the launch that the bike patently needed a steering damper.

Phil West, then road test editor for Bike magazine, was the first to corner the beast on less than perfect British roads, and if Honda's rivals were hoping for a less than enthusiastic showing on Blighty's blighted highways, they were much mistaken. 'The FireBlade steers so quick it's baffling,' wrote West. 'I'm baffled, and judging by all this crap about steering dampers people have been spouting on about recently, I think just about everyone else who's ridden it is baffled too. So let's clarify things a little. The

Steering damper? No, said *Bike* magazine's Phil West when he finally got to ride the FireBlade on less-than-perfect British roads. (Gold and Goose)

CBR's steering is deliciously light. With its KR-1S size trail and 16-inch front wheel it's bound to be; add to the equation light weight and stumpy wheelbase and, yes, twitchy might be an appropriate word. But it's always controllable. It never threatened to tank slap even when a moment's mental aberration meant I once found myself accelerating hard out of a corner on Catseyes. I never had to grasp the bars in a fit of panic, just fun...'

Wootton managed to get hold of a Honda Australia bike in April of that year.

'At Phillip Island the bike looked like being a winner,' he recalls, 'but my major nagging doubt from that Phillip Island foray concerned the FireBlade's stability, as I'd experienced a

AMCN's Ken Wootton rated the bike on the Phillip Island circuit and was surprised to find it stable on the street. (*AMCN*)

couple of head shakes which gave every indication of staining the undies come bumpy public roads. But surprise, surprise that wasn't the case. Perhaps I'd convinced myself that the 16-inch front wheel, Kawasaki KR-1S-type steering geometry and around 30 kilos less weight than the opposition would spell flightiness and tenderness on the street. You can imagine my surprise when the 900 turned out to be a more stable road bike than I'd found on the track. I guess this is because performance on the track is only limited by the capabilities of the bike and the size of one's family jewels, whereas performance on public roads is limited by speed cameras, the boys in blue, and the desire to prolong my stay on this planet. I found the progressive power delivery makes it a really usable bike with surprisingly pleasant road manners. Of course, it's still a very easy bike to do wheelies on if you really want to.'

Other magazines were equally forthcoming of praise. *Performance Bikes* said: 'Every so often someone comes up with a new bike which sets new standards. I cite the Yamaha 350LC, the Suzuki GSX-R, Kawasaki's KR1, the Honda VFR750, early Bimotas and now the FireBlade. The CBR900 is one of those bikes. It can out-brake, out-turn, and out-date every other bike.' The anarchic talents of the *Fast Bikes* road testers, which then housed Emmett – a future GP privateer and later British Superbike star – in their ranks, were also impressed.

'This is the fastest A to B machine in the universe,' they trumpeted. 'If you take off the lights, mirrors and indicators you could qualify for a 500cc Grand Prix.' No-one tested such a claim, but it made the point. The FireBlade was quite simply in a class of its own, and nothing could touch it. And it wasn't just the Brits, either, although many journalists were still unsure as to whether the FireBlade was more like a schizophrenic pit bull terrier or a loyal labrador.

In the USA reaction to the machine was similar. 'The CBR900RR isn't cheap and it isn't perfect,' explained Tim Carrithers of *Motor Cyclist* after testing the first model. 'That 16-inch front-wheel makes steering all too easy and the fork could use a compression-damping adjuster. I could talk all day about mass

centralisation and moments of inertia, but the thing you need to know is that nothing else puts a bigger smile on my face over a twisty bit of road. Absolutely nothing.'

Other *MC* journos had similar feelings.

Nick Ienatsch: 'In the CBR900RR I've found a fantastically fun bike that takes motorcycling a step beyond where it is now with pure function. What happens after that initial step is up to you, but the climb is worth the view.'

Andy Saunders: 'Never mind that the Honda doesn't fit into any specific sportsbike class, the truth is nothing else can compare to the CBR900RR.'

Despite this reaction, the CBR900RR failed to win the *Motor Cyclist* sportsbike test in the summer of 1992. Instead that honour went to the Suzuki GSX-R750 – although it was later found that the CBR900 that *Motorcyclist* had been using did not have enough oil in the forks and the back wheel was out of line.

Elsewhere the FireBlade kept on picking up the honours.

The first group test in the UK was carried out by *Motor Cycle News*. *MCN*'s Chris Dabbs tested the 'Blade against the Yamaha FZR1000RU EXUP and the Suzuki GSX-R1100 and found that the FireBlade took sportsbikes to a new level. 'Once the FireBlade's moving the gap between it and the FZR and GSX-R becomes even wider,' he wrote. 'The Honda is so completely effortless at any speed that it redefines what "good" handling is. Suddenly the slight effort needed to set up the FZR for a bend becomes intolerable and the momentary consideration needed on the GSX-R11 before you aim for the gap ahead in the traffic becomes an absolute pain. On the CBR you just point and go – fast. At the end of the day the FireBlade is the clear winner and probably Bike of the Year. Never mind A to B, it goes from A to Z and back again quicker than the opposition and still manages to be civilised, almost practical everyday transport.'

Performance Bikes tested the CBR900RR against Kawasaki's ZZ-R1100, Yamaha's FZR1000RU EXUP, Suzuki's GSX-R1100N, and Bimota's YB10 Dieci. They took all the bikes round Cadwell Park in Lincolnshire and then went on a road ride taking in the famous 'Cat

Motor Cycle News's Chris Dabbs at the launch. Back in the UK he would be the first to test the FireBlade against its rivals – Yamaha's FZR1000 EXUP and Suzuki's GSX-R1100. It beat both with ease. (*MCN*)

and Fiddle' road between Buxton and Macclesfield.

The CBR came first in braking, scratchability, and personal preference categories, while the ZZ-R won engine, tourability, comfort, value and the overall award score. *PB* admitted they weren't comparing like with like, but they went ahead anyway. They did find a few minor niggles.

'It was measurably faster than anything else at Cadwell so we thought it was a perfect bike. We

had to go a long way (almost to Manchester) before we found anything to criticise. I was surprised to find that when bike and weather were cold it wasn't as much fun flicking the FireBlade from side to side as it was in the bright sunshine at Cadwell just 26 hours before. Also my right hand went numb when the bike stayed at 5,000 revs. On the open road it was necessary to keep the bike over 5,000 anyway. Whereas the other bikes would leap forward at a touch of the throttle in any gear at any speed, the Honda liked the top half of the rev-band. This was all we could find wrong with the bike.'

In other parts of the world it was the same story. At the beginning of 1993 *Australian Motorcycle News* awarded it the prestigious accolade of 'Motorcycle of the Year 1992', saying: 'It's a motorcycle that not only excels at its chosen design brief, but also sets new standards for the class in the way it goes about the task. For once, less is actually more.' So while the bike was well received and adored by many for the way it could give such experienced riders such a large dose of excitement, it was also felt by some that maybe this was just a little too much for the road, and certainly too much for inexperienced riders or the uninitiated.

Kiwi Rider's Jonathan Bentman said of the 1992 machine: 'The 'Blade is the original lean, mean, fighting machine. Built to a never before attained combination of incredible lightness and mind-warping performance, it could even turn on its owners in a sudden fit of tank-slapping after hitting bumps at speed. Innocents were maimed or killed, even experienced riders could find themselves unwitting victims of the 'Blade's brutal demeanour. In my homeland, the UK, it struck a chord with the biking public, bad was good, and the 'Blade – dubbed by some The Assassin – was the baddest most homicidal maniacal pair of wheels available. It became a cult, outselling every other two-wheeler on the English market, mopeds and scooters included.'

It may sound from this as if the FireBlade was downright dangerous, which it wasn't, but unfortunately a tragedy did occur. In March 1992 Peter Bolt, managing editor of *Motor Cycle News*, died on a FireBlade after colliding with a van while riding home from work. Mechanical problems were not to blame for the incident.

Now in the hands of buyers for the first time, this was where the real legend of the Honda CBR900RR FireBlade was forged. Sunday blasts with your best mates took on a whole new meaning as you realised that even a little too much throttle would see the front wheel refuse to touch the ground. When it made

contact with tarmac at last, the thing would turn in quicker than you would have ever thought possible.

Stopping, breathless, you'd try to comprehend what had just happened and explain to your friend what you'd just experienced.

Even the slightest wide-eyed scared comment from one rider to another after a 'moment' was enough to seal it. Word of mouth did the rest and it spread like wildfire, and this sealed the fate of the FireBlade to be the 'baddest mutha' on two-wheels. Whatever adrenaline rushes 'Blade owners were having, others had to have it too, and so the sales, popularity, and infamy of the bike grew.

The thing was, the FireBlade was such a massive leap over the opposition – a feat not seen since the Kawasaki GPZ900R – that it didn't play by other machines' rules. It made up its own. For the uninitiated, this proved to be a problem.

Hancock: 'To be honest, I just think that the original CBR900RR FireBlade was just too flighty for many riders. We looked at that trait and softened it a touch. Nowadays the power-to-weight ratios of bikes are changing all the time. Bikes are getting so light and twitchy. The thing with the FireBlade is that it never really would get out of control. Sure, it would go into a bit of a shimmy if you hit something in the road or even go lock-to-lock in a tank slapper, but it was pretty predictable. During our extensive test programme we found that we could induce the wobble and it would stop. You have the problem when it's not predictable and when you cannot stop the oscillation. That's why we insisted that riders would not need a steering damper for road use with our bike. My favourite out of all the various CBR900RR FireBlade models has to be the original. The first version just gave you a kick like nothing else on the road at the time. I had a black one – it looked so mean, so aggressive.'

In the UK only the extreme sportsbike mag *Fast Bikes* was saying there was nothing wrong with the bike. With a wealth of experienced racer-testers, maybe they could handle it.

Meanwhile, real-world mags were talking about the 'Blade maybe being a bit too sharp.

Launch colours for Europe and the UK were big, bad, butch black or an eye-catching red, white and blue. (Gold and Goose)

Project leader Baba-san also heard the doubts that journalists were voicing over the bike, but was confident of the machine – after all, he'd been proved right about the steering damper after the journalists voiced their concerns at the Phillip Island launch. 'Anyway,' he says, 'a steering damper would have been extra weight.'

Eventually, and with excellent press response across the globe, the sales of the FireBlade began to take off.

Baba-san: 'Just before Easter we received a good response from the market. We were all so pleased. But then right after Easter we had to send out a recall because of a small problem with the disc brake. We were worried that would dent people's belief in the bike. But to our surprise sales didn't fall at all. In Europe and in America, I watched while the 'Blade was accepted by many, many riders. In the end our production line back in Japan had a hectic time, as we had three times more orders for the CBR900RR than we had originally anticipated.'

Ironically, one place that the FireBlade did not get the immediate success it deserved was its homeland of Japan. This was for a variety of reasons. Satoshi Kogure, from the market-leading Japanese motorcycle magazine, *Young Machine*, explains:

'It was at the 1991 Tokyo Motor Show that the

Just as Tadao Baba intended. Journalist Roland Brown demonstrates the 'total control' concept of the CBR. (Roland Brown)

In years to come this name would become synonymous with power and lightness. (Roland Brown)

CBR900RR first appeared before us. The specification made it a big sensation and got us very excited, of course. But we were also surprised, because Honda revealed this export-purposed bike at a domestic show. We guessed this meant that they were very serious about showing a new direction in motorcycles to the Japanese market, even if it would be difficult for the Japanese to actually get hold of them. The first FireBlade was a very good bike. Light, powerful, and exciting. However, it didn't become a very popular bike in Japan for several reasons. First, it was awfully hard to obtain an over-400cc driving licence in Japan at the time; and secondly, when it finally went on sale across the world we had to look for rather limited numbers of re-imported 'Blades from overseas. Circumstances didn't allow the number of Japanese FireBladers to increase that drastically. Plus, the out and out sporty character of the bike meant that it would be strictly for skilled enthusiasts over here.'

Elsewhere the legend was being forged. An unequalled power-to-weight ratio, razor sharp handling, and a competitive price made the overweight opposition look obsolete. And so the accolades kept coming.

It was voted by the readers of *Motor Cycle News* as 'Machine of the Year' in 1993. The bad boys of *Fast Bikes* also made it their 1993 bike of the year. One of France's biggest biking

publications – *Moto Journal* – voted the CBR900RR FireBlade their 'Best Open Class Sportsbike' of 1993. In Europe, 30 of the Continent's top motorcycling magazines voted it 'International Bike of the Year' at the end of 1992.

Meanwhile, performance on the test tracks of Europe also made the FireBlade a world-beater. A number of European magazines, including the *Fast Bikes* team, took the top 18 sportsbikes from around the World to the tough and demanding Mugello circuit in Italy. Even up against the super-expensive and ultra-exotic likes of the Ducati 888SPS and Bimota's futuristic Furano, the bike that recorded the fastest time of the day-long test was none other than the humble, cheap and cheerful (in comparison) CBR900RR FireBlade.

Across the Atlantic, US monthly *Cycle World* made the CBR900RR the best sportsbike of 1993, while up north in the same year, *Cycle Canada* put the FireBlade at the top of their annual competition to find machine of the year. And down-under, *Australian Motorcycle News* voted it the best sportsbike of 1992 – although Kawasaki's ZZ-R1100 won the overall title.

In its launch year of 1992 and then through 1993, the CBR900RR FireBlade had the opposition well and truly licked. And now, through constant scrutiny and development by Honda R&D, it was going to stay there.

Weight watching

For a company that prides itself on its technical prowess, it seems remarkable to think that the FireBlade became a world-beater using just tried and trusted technology. Nothing tricky or fancy was used to make the FireBlade so special. No fuel-injection, no ram-air, no expensive parts made from the latest 'unobtainium', no turbos, no nothing. Well, actually it used a lot of nothing, for that was the secret of the FireBlade – one key ingredient was left out in large amounts. Weight.

Reducing weight enhances the performance of a motorcycle. Generally, the lighter bike will accelerate quicker, needs less of a tug on the brake lever to pull it up, and requires less effort to throw it into a turn.

So, less weight helps, but it also helps if the weight you have is carried in the right places.

Mass centralisation explained. Heavy stuff, like the motor, is close to the centre of gravity, while the extremities are made as light as possible to stop excess weight spoiling the handling. (Honda UK)

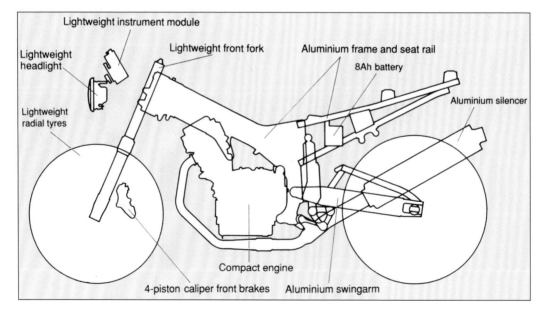

Lightweight instrument module

Lightweight headlight

Lightweight front fork

Aluminium frame and seat rail

8Ah battery

Aluminium silencer

Lightweight radial tyres

Compact engine

4-piston caliper front brakes

Aluminium swingarm

Putting it in the right place is called 'mass-centralisation'. Honda had known about this for a long time, but the four years they had to play on the latest computer aided design (CAD) and computer aided manufacturing (CAM) systems meant that now they could really refine these techniques.

As its name suggests, 'mass centralisation' really *is* about keeping mass centralised. Think about it. If you have something heavy in your hands, like a bowling ball, it's easier to spin around with it held close to you, isn't it? Go for something the same weight as the bowling ball, but with a bulkier mass (like a plank of wood) and it's harder. It's the same with motorcycles. If you can make it lighter, great. If you can't then simply move it nearer to the centre of the machine's mass.

Honda knew this, so all the parts of the FireBlade that sat at the extremities of the design, such as the headlights and instrument cluster, fork sliders, brake calipers, and exhaust end-can, were looked at and scrutinised to see if they could be made lighter. Even such a typically dense item as the battery was made as small as possible (it was a minute 12-volt 8 ampere-hour item, as opposed to the 12-volt 12ah or 14ah units then being used), and was planted as near to the centre of the bike as possible.

However, simply getting the components down to the right weight was just part of the problem, as Baba-san explains: 'We had some hard times. There was some professional conflict between the engineers and the test team over the weight and performance of some parts. Sometimes we achieved an ideal weight, but the quality or durability of the part was affected, so we had to start over again. Let me give you an example. If you want a piece of glass that weighs just 100g, the prototype must start at less than 100g, because as you refine it, it gets heavier. Unfortunately, the first prototype is 200g, so we start working out how we can reduce its weight. After weeks of hard work, we make the 200g prototype 100g and let our test group test it. Then it is found to be too weak, dangerous, ugly, or it cannot do its job properly. We have to abandon the 100g prototype completely, and start all over again from the 200g prototype. Making the 100g glass is not so difficult, but making it to a satisfactory standard is very hard.'

To help with mass-centralisation, Honda engineers have used a device similar to a balance beam since the mid-1970s. The prototype is rolled on to the beam and the engineers watch as the machine finds its natural balance point. Various components can then be moved around the chassis until the desired weight distribution is achieved. The latest CAD/CAM computers can obviously do the same thing – and with much quicker alterations – but, knowing the Japanese, the trusted balance beam is probably still in use somewhere in the depths of Honda Japan…

Obviously, the biggest single component in the CBR900RR was the motor, and the Japanese realised they had to make a pretty compact mill to shoehorn into a positively dainty 1,405mm (55.3in) wheelbase (the distance between front and rear wheel spindles).

First the liquid-cooled, 16-valve motor was to be tilted forward and slanted constant velocity carburettors were used, so every conceivable scrap of space was utilised. A three-chambered airbox was used, which worked by fooling the carbs that they were getting air from a much bigger one. The fuel and air mixture met in the semi-down draught 38mm CV Keihin carbs (just 4mm larger than those fitted to the CBR600), and was shot straight into the combustion chamber through asymmetrically shaped inlet ports, off-set to provide optimum combustion chamber design. The valves were

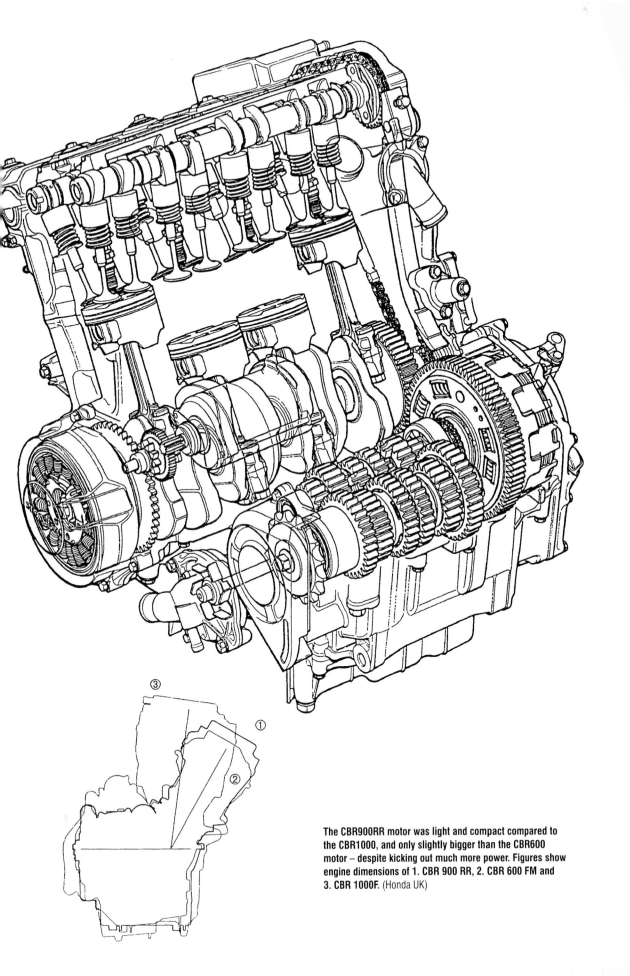

The CBR900RR motor was light and compact compared to the CBR1000, and only slightly bigger than the CBR600 motor – despite kicking out much more power. Figures show engine dimensions of 1. CBR 900 RR, 2. CBR 600 FM and 3. CBR 1000F. (Honda UK)

arranged in a narrow 32° included angle and the asymmetry meant each inlet port had to be a different shape. This did affect peak power, but the Honda engineers felt that the compact dimensions and a strong mid-range were more important than the sacrifice of a peaky power delivery.

The engine itself had bore and stroke figures of 70mm and 58mm. Generally, the longer the stroke of a motor – all other factors being equal – the more mid-range power the motor will produce at the expense of power at the top-end of the rev-range. For a given displacement, the longer the stroke the smaller the pistons and therefore a smaller combustion area and less valve area. The long stroke of the motor and slimmer, lighter pistons in the engine actually make a much narrower motor possible.

In the actual construction of the motor no expensive alloys or carbon-fibre were used. Instead, an evolution of existing practices and materials gave the engine a hallmark of light weight and high power.

The cam chain was placed on the right-hand side of the engine to cut down on width, and the one-piece crankcase and cylinder barrels meant that weight was also saved. All four bores were squeezed as close together as possible to cut down on width, and certain parts, such as the front sprocket cover, were made of plastic rather than dense and heavy metal. Other things, such as the lack of an adjustable gear linkage, a lightweight water pump housing, and a tiny but powerful alternator, meant the FireBlade had a class-leading, lightweight heart.

Depending on which dyno you believe, the CBR mill was pumping out around 110–120bhp at 10,500rpm, just 500rpm from the redline and 1,000 short of the rev-limiter.

All in all the motor weighed in at 65kg (143.2lb), only 6kg (13.2lb) heavier than its little brother, the CBR600, and 15kg (33lb) less than its rival – Yamaha's FZR1000RU EXUP motor. Added to this, it was only 13mm (0.5in) taller than Honda's own CBR600 motor and just 50mm (2in) wider. The basic layout of both engines was very similar, and that's not an accident. The CBR900RR, including the motor, was ready *before* the CBR600. Honda decided to hold the FireBlade back for a year or so and use spin-off technology from the 900 programme to help make the re-designed CBR600F the world-beater that it became in 1991.

The 'Blade's chassis was also designed with lightness in mind. Again, CAD/CAM calculations meant that the main frame's combination of forgings, castings, stampings, and extrusions weighed in at just 10.5kg (23.1lb). The removable rear sub-frame was also manufactured from lightweight box-section aluminium. The cast steering head was welded to two large extruded spars, which featured four internal strengthening ribs. They met a complex casting which held the rear engine mounts and swingarm pivot.

At the back end Honda could have used its patented single-sided Pro-Arm rear suspension, as used on the RC30 and VFR750 at the time. Sure, it would have looked really trick, but the penalty for this bit of kit was excessive weight. Instead, the CBR used a lighter, conventional looking double sided arm. Technology from Honda's NSX supercar programme helped the CBR engineers to shape the upper swingarm brace as it's extruded (pulled), as opposed to shaping it after extrusion. This preserves the strength of the metal, as the original molecular structure of the aluminium is maintained.

At the front end of the machine, current fashion in 1992 (and still, in some ways, today) was that upside-down or inverted forks were the way to go. With motocross machines and, latterly, road race machines switching to

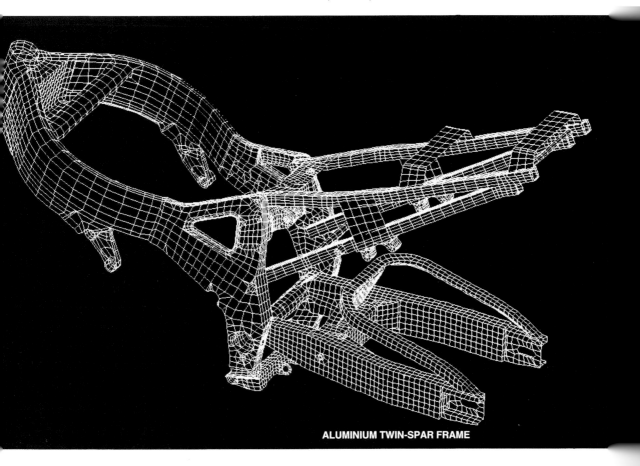

CAD/CAM illustration shows the bare bones of the 'Blade.
(Honda UK)

ALUMINIUM TWIN-SPAR FRAME

inverted front forks, many manufacturers – including Kawasaki, Suzuki, and Yamaha – immediately followed suit with their road-going race-replica range. But Honda and Baba-san refused.

Inverted forks are generally a little heavier than their right-way-up counterparts, and also the heavier part is at the end of the fork where it joins the front wheel spindle. Remember, weight at the extremities is bad for mass-centralisation.
So Honda went with a conventional set of forks instead, but these too were scrutinised to save weight.

Instead of using orthodox cast and machined aluminium, engineers found that an extruded ally tube screwed and glued into a cast steel end-piece weighed in at just 900g. The walls of the CBR900RR's 45mm diameter forks are just 2mm thick, compared to the race-bred RC30's 43mm front forks which are 2.3mm.

Just in case they might lose sales to bikes with inverted telescopic forks, the finished product was then made to look like a 'fashionable' upside-down front fork.

Both wheels were also lightweight aluminium-alloy U-spoke items, and the Nissin brakes were small, four-piston arrangements biting into light 296mm discs.

Even the not-so-vital parts were given the

Lightweight clocks surrounded by race-like foam rather than 'heavy' plastic sat in front of lightweight lenses. (Honda UK)

lightweight/mass-centralisation treatment. The end-can was formed from aluminium rather than steel and impact-extruded to combine lighter weight with greater strength. The instruments were made up of a speedometer and tachometer held in lightweight foam rather than sturdy plastic. Below them hung exposed wires for the headlights that sat behind lightweight plastic (instead of glass) lenses.

Many of the qualities and comforts afforded to VFR/CBR owners in the past were dropped in an attempt to make the machine lighter. It all worked, but many owners would complain that, compared to other CBR models, the FireBlade sacrificed an overall good finish in its crusade against weight.

But that was not Honda's primary concern. As long as it could compete finish-wise with the competition, that was enough – and it did. Instead, less weight, compactness, and power

were the main driving forces behind the design, and it worked. In the UK's first comparison test between the CBR and its big-bore sports rivals in *Motor Cycle News*, the 'Blade had a dry weight of 185kg (407.5lb) and 113bhp against the Yamaha FZR1000 EXUP's 214kg (471.4lb) and 117.5bhp and the mighty Suzuki GSX-R1100's 251kg (552.9lb) and 132bhp. That gave it a class leading power-to-weight ratio of 0.61bhp per kilo, compared to the Yamaha's 0.55bhp/kilo and the Suzuki's 0.53bhp/kilo. Allied to this was a tiny wheelbase that looked as if it belonged on a kid's bicycle. All the space saving resulted in a 1,405mm (55.3in) wheelbase, compared to the EXUP's 1,470mm (57.9in), and the Suzuki's 1,535mm (60.4in). Scarier still was the thought that the FireBlade was even shorter than its little brother the CBR600, which possessed a 1,409.7mm (54.5in) wheelbase.

1994 FireBlade – foxeye power…

Good as the 1992 and 1993 FireBlades were, Honda realised that they could not afford to rest on their laurels. So for 1994 (1995 in the USA) the Flying Wing gave the CBR its first big upgrade.

From the front of the bike you could see that there had been some changes. Instead of the two separate headlights the 1994–5 FireBlade wore a sleeker one-piece reflector headlight, in a style which was to become known as 'foxeye'. As well as giving the machine an all-new look, the new set-up was 20 per cent lighter than the old 'Blade's eyes. The multi-reflector headlights worked by bouncing light focused from the bulbs backwards on to a polished reflective surface which scattered the beam ahead. The headlights sat in a redesigned upper fairing, held by a lighter aluminium fairing stay. The fairing was 20mm (0.8in) wider than the old one and with a screen which was 15mm (0.6in) taller to keep a little more of the windblast off the rider. Inside, the fairing hid updated electronic instruments (300g/10.5oz lighter) with a new idiot light arrangement, and the new electronic speedo was fed from a sensor unit rather than a traditional cable.

More weight was saved (another 300g) from the cylinder head being magnesium rather than aluminium.

More important changes centred around the two areas where the original 'Blade suffered most criticism – front suspension and the gear shift arrangement.

Honda redesigned the gear shift linkage on the later model and the change meant an end to the annoying 'clunk' that greeted owners of the original bike on an up or downchange. Also of help were the re-angled shift cogs, a lighter gear lever return, and shift drum stopper springs. All these changes added up to a much more positive feel.

Up front bigger changes were made. The 45mm cartridge-type Showa forks looked similar to their predecessors, but almost everything inside was revamped in a bid to lose the FireBlade's 'flighty front-end' image.

At the end of the longer tubes sat new click-stop compression damping adjusters which, hopefully in the standard position of six clicks from maximum, were an improvement over the harsh feel of the previous 'legs'. The 1994–5 forks carried 38 per cent less compression than the earlier units, along with 10 per cent more rebound damping over a far broader range of adjustment. The dual rate fork springs were also firmer. At the rear, the Showa shock's spring rate was identical to the earlier model, although the damper got 20 per cent more rebound damping and roughly 33 per cent more on the compression side for a much more smooth action and return.

The silencer was now made of a flashy brushed aluminium, and the CBR's camshafts nestled under lightweight magnesium covers. The internal cam chain was beefed up, as were the clutch plates, and under the seat there was now a special place reserved for a U-lock. Practicality as well as performance.

All these changes made for a better bike and one that was just *one pound* (less than half a kilo) heavier than its forebear.

1996 FireBlade – more comfort, more capacity, more fun

Honda made big changes to the 1996 FireBlade, even though the 1994-6 machines looked very similar. In general, power was up (thanks to a bigger-bore), weight was down, and the sum of the parts was a package that was much more comfortable and easier to ride.

Power was up by around 4–6bhp – the figure ranged from 123bhp to 128 at the crank at 10,500rpm, depending on whose dyno you believed. This was due to a minimal 0.10 point compression ratio rise, and a significant 1mm overbore. The 1996 CBR displaced 918.5cc, taking the motor 25cc up on the previous model.

For 1994–5 the cast-in cylinder liners lost their flanges and rough surface finishes. Instead, a new casting technique allowed non-flanged, smooth finished liners, thus allowing Honda to overbore each cylinder without increasing the motor's overall width. In fact the width was brought down, narrowed 9.5mm (0.4in) with a new, more compact generator which used a new exotic magnetic compound in its construction.

The bigger, only very slightly heavier pistons, were matched to larger connecting rods with bigger crankshaft big end journals to match. The cylinder head cover was also now made from lighter magnesium rather than alloy. The gearbox was reworked to lessen the gaps between first through third gears, and to provide a higher overall sixth gear. To take off a little more weight, the drive chain was reduced in size from a 530 chain to a 525.

Ignition was now three-dimensionally mapped. This is a system that wasn't available when the 'Blade first came out in 1992, and works by tailoring ignition to various rpm and engine regimes. Its introduction meant that the motor could be a little more flexible without the added cost of either fuel-injection or the variable valve timing that Honda use on much of its car range. The silencer was still brushed alloy but one litre up in size, to six litres. All in all the motor – for all these improvements – was just 200g heavier.

A whole list of parts had been lightened, including the tyres. The new Bridgestone BT56F and 56R Battlaxes (replacing the BT50) were designed to help them get to their optimum operating temperature sooner. They were of dual-compound construction – hard in the middle where you spend most of your time and soft on the edges where you want the real grip. The 56s also featured a new tread pattern claimed to optimise cornering grip.

Design of the frame and swingarm on the 1996 model left sections of the frame 'open-backed', instead of closed; this helped reduce weight. The frame was a triple-box section, instead of quad-box section as before, but was claimed to be more rigid in critical areas – although Baba-san actually made the new frame less rigid in places, finding, after extensive research, that for road use a little flex is actually beneficial for rider feedback. Honda engineers insisted that lateral (side to side) strength was not compromised by this 'dialled-in' flex or the open-backed frame design.

A new, curved radiator kept the same cooling area but with less width and weight. There were also smaller, lighter indicators ('turn signals' in the USA). The conventional front suspension, consisting of compression damping, rebound, and preload adjustment,

All change for 1996 – but you'd hardly notice it. Motor was 200g lighter and overall weight was down 2kg (4.4lb). (Gold and Goose)

had been reworked and trimmed for lightness. The biggest change to the front forks was that the old system of oil passing through shims was replaced by the fork oil passing through drilled holes in discs. Baba-san and his team discovered that shims worked well on motocross machines, when there is lots of oil sloshing about and therefore lots of suspension travel, but on a road bike, with maybe four or five inches of travel, the drilled disc system worked much more progressively and smoothly. This meant that when the bike hit a bump or accelerated hard, the fluid would pass more gradually through the fork, meaning there was less of a tendency to transfer weight backwards and forwards so rapidly. The system was called HMAS, standing for 'Honda multi-action system'. Holding the forks in place were new triple clamps. Rear suspension had also been altered, again using the HMAS system. It also had a smaller diameter piston, claimed to give a greater range of adjustments, and a reworked linkage ratio giving more progressive damping over a longer amount of travel.

To thrash? or not to thrash?

Excellently put together though they were (they're Hondas after all…), a new 'Blade, nevertheless presented each owner with a problem. Should he or she thrash it from new, or follow the owners' manual's running-in procedures to the letter?

The problem was that one school of thought said that you shouldn't subject the motor to too much hardship too soon, while others said the design tolerances and modern materials were so good that if you thrashed it right from the off the bike would loosen up nicely and give you lots of extra power.

Magazines across the world reported on CBRs giving anything from 104–128bhp as standard – bizarre! People then started talking about 'good' FireBlades and 'duff' ones. Not that the 'duff' ones were that duff, they just seemed down on power for some reason.

Bike magazine dynoed one of the first 'Blades in the country in 1992 and found an impressive 124bhp at the back wheel when Honda themselves were only quoting 122. One year later a FireBlade was dynoed just before a group test on the Isle of Man and it made just 112bhp. Other magazines were getting lower figures.

Ray Stringer has spent years racing superbikes and production bikes successfully both in the UK and internationally, and he now runs his own race team. He's seen plenty of FireBlades and countless other modern sportsbikes on his dyno and he is in no doubt as to the best course of action.

'I think you should thrash the living daylights out of them from day one,' he says. 'From what I have seen, modern production machines loosen up that bit better if they've been given a hard life right from the very beginning. Bikes that are run in to the manual do loosen up, but they still end up a little tight and a few horsepower down.'

Ray has seen many first-generation FireBlades on his dyno to back up his claim.

According to some tuners, thrashing the 'Blade could liberate some extra brake horsepower…

He says: 'A couple of guys have brought in early 1992 to 1994 CBR900RRs to be dynoed, and they've admitted they gave the bike a lot of stick from brand new. These machines have seen anything up to 125bhp at the back wheel, where properly run-in new FireBlades might struggle to make 110–115bhp. This method has been borne out by us with our production race bikes over the years. Ignore the manual and the bike loosens up nicely. When I competed in the Suzuki GSX-R cup in 1988-9 we were all given machines straight from the crate which had only just had their pre-delivery inspection [PDI] and we were told to thrash them around the track – without running them in. The factory said that was fine. If you speak to many manufacturers, secretly they will say that nowadays the "running-in" period is more of a safety thing with the rider. A stepped running-in period gets the rider into the performance of the machine nice and gradually rather than letting him or her redline such a big powerful machine in every gear right from the off.'

Increased comfort was a byword for the '96 bike and this was helped by 10mm higher clip-ons than the previous bike and a seat height also increased by 10mm to give the rider just a little more legroom. Also, the tank was reshaped for more rider room.

All together the changes added up to a lot – even if the bike didn't look that much different.

Enthusiasts noticed the 'gills' in the tail-unit and the new front mudguard/fender with holes that (it was claimed) aided aerodynamics, shielded the fork legs from copping too much road debris, and simultaneously directed air into the new radiator. Slightly more slippery aerodynamics on the upper fairing also helped top speed just a tad.

1998 FireBlade – 'Blade blunted?

For 1998, Honda again changed the technical makeup of the FireBlade and again improved the breed – although this time it faced its sternest test in the shape of the Kawasaki ZX-9RC1 Ninja and the Yamaha YZF-R1. The CBR900RR's development team wanted to further refine the overall balance between lighter weight and making the machine more comfortable to ride at speed and for longer periods. Remember how the CBR1000F went from sportsbike to sports tourer? Honda weren't quite going that far (how can you, with a bike called the FireBlade?), but refinement meant comfort.

To this end, time in the wind tunnel led to the redesigning of the upper fairing to further protect the rider's hands (now on bars set a few millimetres higher still, and a little wider) and upper body, helping to improve comfort and minimise riding fatigue. Despite the protection offered by the slightly wider fairing, work in the wind tunnel showed that the new design was actually more streamlined than the previous model's more blunt front end.

It still looked like a FireBlade, though. The bike's dual multi-reflector headlight was even modified to give the 'foxeyes' a more sinister 'scowl'. Under the eyes nestled a wide, gaping, but at the moment blanked off air scoop, through which – said the magazine rumour mongers – the 'Blade would be breathing through a pukka ram-air system at the turn of the century.

Design-wise, the bike's wide fuel tank and middle and lower fairing cowls were left untouched, although the seat and tail cowl were subtly redesigned with a slightly wider profile, losing the previous model's 'fish gills' in the tail unit. At the back end of the bike was housed a smoother shaped rear light. More subtle yet important changes had been undertaken in the engine department. Capacity was unchanged at 918.5cc, but computer assisted engineering (CAE) was used extensively to extract small improvements in the engine's efficiency and performance. No major modifications were made to the engine's fundamental design – such major components as the crankshaft, connecting rods, and camshafts were left untouched – but modifications were made to 80 per cent of its internals. The shapes of the combustion chambers and the intake and exhaust ports were all carefully refined to reduce air flow resistance for quicker, sharper throttle response. Although the '98 model's 38mm CV-type carbs and air filter were identical to the '97 model, the carburettors' vacuum piston size was changed in order to react to the throttle opening quicker and therefore provide stronger acceleration from any speed. Further inside the motor the bores shared composite cylinder sleeves as used on the race-bred RVF RC45 and the new-for-'98 model VFR800.

These sleeves weighed 640g, lighter than the steel items they replaced, and were manufactured from sintered aluminium powder impregnated with ceramic and graphite. As well as being lighter, the new sleeves helped to expel heat quicker and more efficiently.

Each of the four pistons featured a lightweight, low-friction design for top performance, and were coated with a new 'LUB-Coat' solid lubricant which helped minimise friction between the piston and the cylinder wall.

The FireBlade's three-dimensional map-type

The 1998 'Blade was better still. Less weight, more trail, and a longer frame but with a similar wheelbase, stabilised the machine somewhat. But many felt it was blunted. (Gold and Goose)

digital ignition system was reprogrammed with a new timing map that took advantage of the engine's reduced internal friction and the modifications to the combustion chambers and ports, to help give precise response, optimal performance and acceleration, and smoother transitions throughout the rev range.

To reduce mass for sharper acceleration, the '98 FireBlade featured a new, more compact clutch. Its friction disc material allowed the use of fewer plates – down from ten to eight – while maintaining the same performance and reliability (although some magazines criticised this change while conducting stressful quarter-mile times during tests that made the clutches go 'pop').

Refinements to the powertrain and gear ratios helped ensure that the updated motor was performing at the best of its ability throughout the engine's peak rev range. Likewise, a 3.3 per cent increase in the top gear ratio, combined with the engine's stronger performance, helped the bike attain higher top speeds, more comfortable cruising at lower revs, and reduced fuel consumption.

To keep the bike cool at high operating temperatures the volume of its radiator was increased by adding another row to the core, which gave it 7 per cent more cooling capacity along with increased cooling capability, and small but significant improvements to the engine's coolant circulation helped ensure stable performance under a widely varying range of ambient temperature conditions.

The 1998 FireBlade's exhaust system was now made entirely of stainless steel tubing, stretching from the engine's exhaust ports all the way to the flange of its lightweight impact-extruded aluminium canister-style silencer. The silencer's volume was increased by 5 per cent, reducing exhaust resistance for a sharper power output. Although longer, it was also lighter than the 1997-spec unit it replaced.

The 16-inch front wheel

One of the most controversial aspects of the
ground-breaking Honda CBR900RR FireBlade was
the use of that 16-inch front wheel. At the time, 17-
inchers were *de rigueur* for sports-based
motorcycles – even the Kawasaki GPz900R, a
previous sportsbike king, had made the switch from
a 16-inch front to a 17 a few years previously. But
Honda wanted something a little different, to make
the FireBlade turn in to corners that little bit
quicker.

Honda engineers wanted the rolling diameter of a
low profile 17-inch wheel for optimum steering, but
also the lower weight and lower gyroscopic effect
of a 16-inch front wheel. To do this they teamed up
with Japanese tyre giant Bridgestone to come up
with a solution.

Bridgestone designed a special 16-inch radial
tyre, made from the same sticky track compound
rubber but with the circumference of a low-profile
17-incher. The wheel and tyre design meant that a
front radial had to have a taller than normal 70 per
cent aspect ratio of a bias belted tyre. To make this
happen Bridgestone incorporated two opposing
piles of Kevlar-type material into the tyres' belting.
The end result is a tyre with a much steeper curve
to the tread than a 'normal' radial – and thus
quicker steering. The extra weight of the bigger tyre
was more than offset by the reduced mass of the
smaller and lighter front wheel.

Even the rear tyre had a bit of lard cut from it, by
only having a single ply rather than the normal two.
This kept the rear hoop's weight down to just 5.5kg
(12.1lb).

Opinion was divided over the choice. Some road
testers liked the set-up while others felt a return to
a 17-inch front would cure the early FireBlade's
tendency to be a little flighty at the front-end.

Early racing FireBlades – such as the Two
Brothers Racing CBR900RR in the USA – had to
switch to an RC30 front wheel to get sticky 17-inch
rubber, as in early 1992 only Bridgestone and
Michelin made race rubber to fit. Erion Racing's
championship-winning machines have stuck with
the 17-inch front wheel set-up ever since.
On its road bikes Honda stuck with the 16-inch
front wheel for seven years, before finally
succumbing to the lure of a steadier 17-inch front.
Honda being Honda, if you asked an engineer the
reason why, none would say this was an
admittance of the fact that they were wrong, but
more an acknowledgement of the fact that progress
demands change.

**Love it or hate it, this 16-inch diameter piece of rubber has
been the cause of a lot of debate in sportsbike circles since
1992.** (Honda UK)

In the quest of achieving the 'holy grail' of lighter weight and sharper performance, the FireBlade's chassis and frame also received minute yet extensive modifications. These included detailed changes in the thicknesses of the frame's main components, to increase strength in key areas and further optimise its balance of rigidity while reducing weight wherever possible. Combined with modifications to the engine, weight gains that resulted from the strengthening of certain components were counterbalanced by weight losses elsewhere produced a total overall weight saving of 3kg (6.6lb).

In the interests of achieving more stable handling, the frame's steering head stem was moved forward 5.5mm (0.2in) (as measured from the swingarm pivot) and compensated for by a 5mm reduction in front fork offset (from 35mm to 30, or 1.4in to 1.2), resulting in a 5mm increase in trail that did not affect steering rake or wheelbase figures. This led to a claimed improvement in road feel, as well as less fatigue for a rider taking his 'Blade along bumpy town roads.

With its hybrid construction front fork, the 1998 FireBlade's suspension remained essentially the same. Fork springs and damping settings were slightly modified for an enhanced feeling of control.

Other changes included a 10mm (0.4in) wider fork span that helped achieve a 10 per cent increase in the fork's torsional rigidity. Although the triple-clamps and their related parts were larger in size, they were also lighter in weight owing to the replacement of the previous model's steel lower triple-clamp and stem in favour of lightweight aluminium.

The rear suspension featured an all-new tapered box-section aluminium swingarm, widest where it was connected to the strong, cast aluminium cross-brace, gradually tapering back to axle holders and forward to the swingarm pivot. Like the '97 model, the swingarm was supported by a remote reservoir rear damper that offered a wide range of adjustability and a more smoothly controlled ride.

Braking was now provided by new opposed four-piston front brake calipers, combined with larger diameter 310mm floating discs (up from the 1996–7 model's 296mm rotors) to offer easier control and greater resistance to fade. The rear brake was the same single-piston caliper unit used on the previous model.

As if all these improvements weren't enough, Honda R&D even looked at the clocks for weight-saving ideas. The 1998 model's one-piece instrument cluster was only 28mm (1.1in) thick and featured a fully integrated electronic meter panel which meant it was lighter and more compact for easier positioning within the cockpit area, adding to a cleaner look. It featured a flexible thin-film printed circuit 'board' for simplified construction and easy connection by way of a single modular plug. The panel included a large, centralised tachometer with speedometer positioned on the left, new digital LCD temperature gauge and odometer/trip meter, and a standard set of idiot lights.

Still on top, still number one. Nick Jefferies – 1993 F1 TT winner – lofts a 1996 'Blade over the mountain at Cadwell Park, Lincolnshire. (Jason Critchell)

Honing the 'Blade

The swordsmith would continually 'turn' the hot blade, hammering it over on itself time and time again to rid the steel of impurities.

Honda had won. The flying wing had produced a world beater which the bike buying public feared, respected, and enjoyed in equal measure and would, over the coming years, buy in their tens of thousands.

But the competition wasn't going to lie down and take it. In 1993 the 750cc race rep category was still a pretty fierce market place, with Kawasaki releasing the much improved (and now full power) ZXR750L1, Yamaha finally replacing the outdated limited-edition FZR750R OW01 with the mass-market YZF750, and Honda updating its own VFR750 for 1994. Suzuki were still stuck with their double-cradle framed GSX-R750 (now in WP guise for 1993), but a long-in-the-tooth chassis and engine combination meant that despite it being the best GSX-R for years, it couldn't match the newer Kawasaki or Yamaha models.

Despite these machines losing out 150cc to the CBR, all the claimed power figures for the 'sportier' of the 750s were hovering close to the 124bhp region claimed for the 'Blade.

The 750s also had something the 'Blade didn't have at the time – a racing pedigree.

Sure, the FireBlade had attitude and a fearsome reputation, but at the time interest in superbike racing, both at home and abroad, meant that there was a certain coolness turning up at a race on a YZF or ZXR, only to watch bikes with silhouettes identical to your own machine hurtle through the bends at breakneck speeds.

With years of constant refinement the Kawasaki ZXR750L1 of 1993–4 was a formidable machine. That hallmark Kawasaki grunt came from the ram-aired and now full power liquid-cooled inline four (in 1991–2 Kawasaki insisted on building the neutered 100bhp J-series in a bid to second-guess the then threatening 100bhp Euro law), while the chassis – developed as it was on the world's

Kawasaki's 1994 ZXR750. Top front end, nice styling – but not quite the big-bore cigar. (Kawasaki UK)

race circuits – boasted the sharpest handling front-end in the business. Think which direction you want to go in and the ZXR would take you there, almost before you'd decided. Also, compared to the still flighty 'Blade, the ZXR's razor front end would faultlessly track over every bump and ripple with barely a murmur.

Power was there (121bhp was claimed) and it was rough and ready – one of the attractions of a Kawasaki powerplant – but the mid-range was lacking. There was also the problem of weight. Sure, the ZXR was heaps better than its predecessor, but the L1 model was also lardier, some 10 kilos (22lb) lardier. It seemed that Kawasaki could do everything except put their machines on a calorie-controlled diet.

Being an all-new model, the YZF was closer to the FireBlade in overall performance and was also boasting a claimed 124bhp (two more than the CBR), but in reality it generally produced less where it really mattered – at the rear wheel on the dyno.

A trick little gizmo the YZF did have up its sleeve was the mid-range boosting EXUP power valve. Yamaha had used the it on the majority of its important sports machines to date. The FZR1000 Genesis received the EXUP valve back in 1989, and was forever known as the EXUP thereafter (as well as becoming the best-selling big sports machine in the early part of the 1990s); the race FZR750R OW01used it to take on Honda's V4 RC30 on shop floors, if not the race track; and the jewel-like FZR400RR also had the valve, as did a number of later machines including the Thunderace and YZF-R1.

This seminal piece of Yamaha technology is sited at the end of the down pipes and is a butterfly valve which at low revs closes to create back pressure, stopping gases escaping too quickly and fooling the engine into thinking it has shorter header pipes, thus boosting power. As the revs rise, the valve shuts the other way, giving maximum power before the redline.

This meant the YZF had a useful mid-range advantage over the ZXR, and almost, just, could keep up with an angry 'Blade. But what it didn't have was the kick-in-the-pants top end rush that the CBR900RR and even the growling ZXR delivered.

Chassis wise the YZF was a corker – even if it did sacrifice some of the tricker cycle parts compared to its predecessor, the limited run OW01.

One of the first big tests for the CBR900RR and these racy 750 machines was when *Bike* magazine took them all to the Isle of Man. FireBlades actually racing around the legendary 37.73-mile circuit was still some three years off (see Chapter 5) but this was the next best thing: all the major players on the harshest test of all – and on 'Mad Sunday.'

It was a close thing, as Phil West explained: 'Even after two weeks and 1,000 miles on the YZF, CBR, and ZXR, there's no clear cut answer to the "which is best" riddle. What is certain is this: the YZF is a Swiss watch among sportsbikes. It's the slickest, sweetest, most neutral, deceptively fast and easy to get on with race replica yet. But next to the rough diamond, no compromise ZXR it's also a bit of an all-rounder. Slightly soft, slightly baggy, and (very) antiseptic. So where does that leave the FireBlade? Up front on the back wheel and with its rider giggling like someone possessed, that's where. For all its front-end friskiness, for all its power-drive bonkers-ness, the FireBlade remains motorcycling's number one good time toy. It might not be as pure round corners as the ZXR. It might not be as accomplished, able and massively impressive as the YZF, but what it has is excitement – and an outrageous amount of it.'

The 750s just didn't have the real killer punch to take on the FireBlade. They excelled in certain areas, but as an overall package and for the price, they couldn't match the CBR.

But rumours soon started circulating in the world's press about a Kawasaki that just might be able to take on the FireBlade. Journalists said that there was a ZXR900 coming for 1994, which would combine the best elements of the ZXR750 – which was generally accepted to have the best steering and front-end in the race-replica class – and the good bits of the mighty Kawasaki ZZ-R1100, which meant the stonking 178mph (286kph) motor.

900s are the 'class of '94'

Despite all that was going on, the CBR900RR remained unchanged for the 1993 season. However, Honda's belief in small improvements to develop the breed meant that the best would get better. And get better it did, with a makeover for 1994.

Dave Hancock from Honda UK hadn't finished his association with the FireBlade just because it had a successful launch at the end of 1992. In fact his relationship with the big CBR was only just beginning.

'As with many other of Honda's bikes, development of the new FireBlade started about a year after the original came out,' he

If only slightly modified, it still looked damned aggressive. The 1994 FireBlade with its 'foxeye' headlamps. (Honda UK)

recalls. 'In the year after the CBR's launch I was still heavily involved in charting how the bike was received. We'd obviously listen to what the new owners were saying about the bike and we'd have regular quality check meetings. Initial changes to the 'Blade were limited to colour, cosmetic and minor details, but soon we were getting information back from the customers via the dealers and servicing that they loved the bike but wanted it to be a little

milder and a little easier to ride.'

One of the only two major criticisms Hancock was hearing was that the gearbox didn't seem up to the normal high Honda standards. At best it could be described as average. Press and public alike complained of a notchy 'box which needed a firm prod of the boot to change gear, not something you want to be thinking of when you're travelling at FireBlade speed.

Okay, said Honda, and upgraded it to take

away the unpredictability of changing gear by means of a revised linkage system and internal mods.

In came upgraded front forks, too, as press and owners felt that the original CBR still seemed a little harsh at the front end. Compared to the old 45mm items Honda now made the '94 'Blade's fully adjustable, adding compression damping to the forks. The journalists reckoned this helped a lot, even if in

many riding regimes these changes might not actually make the bike feel any different. And to Honda they were part of corporate, professional pride in improving the breed.

That so, shaving a further – and surely negligible – 0.3kg (0.7lb) by swapping the old model's aluminium cylinder head for a magnesium one, must border on the obsessive.

But the real change was the styling. Honda

had kept a keen eye on the opposition. It had seen that separate headlights à la ZXR750 and old 'Blade were now a little passé, and that the new trend was more towards flush-fit lights which blended in with the wind tunnel induced curves that were the norm for sportsbikes.

'Foxeye' was the name for the vulpine lilt in the shape of the headlights, behind which hid a new multi-reflector headlight design. There were practical rather than cosmetic changes, too. Although it was hard to spot, there was a slightly larger, more protective upper fairing, beneath which nestled a redesigned instrument binnacle.

Despite the change, the CBR still had the aggressive looks of the original 'Blade – and it retained the gossamer weight of the original along with the atom-bomb delivery of that stupendous engine.

The whole CBR again managed to add up to more than the sum of its parts, with the 27 changes between the old and new models really refining the bike.

In 1994 the 750 class had few changes. Instead a number of additions came in on the 900 class.

Newest of the kids was the much-heralded ZX-9R Ninja (not the ZXR900, as first thought). Kawasaki could lay claim to inventing the 900cc bandwagon – thanks to the Z1 from the 1970s, and the ground-breaking GPz900R in the '80s. As it turned out, it may have had a sexy name like the FireBlade, but it was also carrying a few too many pounds to seriously threaten the CBR's dominance. Still, the ZX-9's time would come.

For crude comparison, the 'Blade weighed in at just 185kg (407.5lb), compared to Kawasaki's newly introduced ZX-9R, which was a portly 215kg (473.61lb).

As suspected, the Ninja had a stonking, ram-air boosted motor which, with 125 *restricted* bhp on tap, trounced the 'Blade's 115–122bhp. But the extra lard sat uneasily on the Ninja's shoulders – as did talk at the launch of handling problems with the bike's soft rear end. Even when de-restricted to 137bhp the ZX-9R was still considered to be more sports-tourer than sports. Road tests described the bike feeling more like its big

Ducati's stunning 916. As beautiful and as sharp as a Cavalier's jewelled rapier – but also as expensive. (Ducati)

brother ZZ-R1100 than its sportier sibling the ZXR750 – despite the fact that it had more in common with the latter.

A 'real-world' bike, said some. Quite. But who wants to be reminded of the real world?

Moving further away from the real world, 1994 also offered a new machine at the more exotic end of the race-replica range. If you wanted exclusivity, you could spend your money on Ducati's new and extremely gorgeous 916. Being a Ducati it was obviously more expensive than the Honda (at £11,800, it was £3,605 more than the FireBlade's £8,195) and also more desirable.

People were drooling over the 916, and rightly so. After riding one, Phil West from *Bike* said: 'I was simply stunned. It's the 'Bike of the Year' 1994 (and, in all likelihood, the bike of 1995 and 1996 too). It's really the first Ducati that you don't have to make "Italian charisma" type excuses for.'

Also released for that model year was a 900 sportsbike for the Anglophiles – Triumph's Daytona 900 Super III. It might have been a nod to the direction the Hinckley-based factory wanted to go in the future with newer models (they'd only been selling machines for three years at the time), but it wasn't a FireBlade beater and probably not expected to be. Respected engineering firm Cosworth had tinkered with the internals and Triumph had dispensed with a small amount of weight by shaving off a little here and there, such as with a carbon-fibre mudguard. Add to all this the price tag of £9,699 and you could see it wasn't playing the same game.

Suzuki also had a new 900 out that year, the RF900. It had a stoater of a motor, claiming 125bhp at 10,000rpm. It seemed to be playing the ZX-9R's game more than the 'Blade's, as it weighed in at 203kg (447.1lb). Where it did win was on price. In February 1994 a ZX-9R cost £8,095 compared to the RF's £6,799 – a good saving, although the finish and equipment level of the bike showed just where Suzuki had made the savings.

Whereas the 1994 750s didn't have the overall performance to take on the FireBlade, both the ZX-9R Ninja and the 916 promised to at least be in the same ballpark. The specification of the Kawasaki Ninja hinted that it was playing a slightly different game. Whereas a 'Blade carried just 185kg (407.5lb), the ZX-9R was a full 30kg (66.1lb) heavier. The motor was a monster in the fullest Kawasaki tradition, but one thing really hamstrung the big Kawasaki.

After the Malaysian launch of the Ninja, a number of magazines were highly critical of the rear end of the bike. The most vocal of these in the UK was *Fast Bikes*, whose deputy editor Dan Harris – later a national class racer and *Superbike* staffer – immediately criticised the rear end for being too soft and sloppy for track and fast road use.

Aussie MCN's editor, the legendary Kenneth Wootton, agreed: 'The earlier B model ZX-9R Ninjas always had heaps of go, but getting it to the tarmac could be a pretty fraught experience.'

In normal road use, the ZX-9R was a fantastic bike, but with riders of the calibre of some of the journalists, the rear end problem left them leaving long dark lines coming out of the corners.

Kevin Ash from *MCN* attended the launch and found that back home the rear-end felt much better. 'At the launch at a very hot Shah Alam race track the rear suspension was just too soft. When we managed to get a ZX-9R back in the UK the feeling was much improved. The rear just felt that much firmer. It may have been the viscosity of the oil in the rear shock, or the fact that harsh track abuse was just too much for it. It still wasn't perfect, but it was heaps better.'

During the four-year lifespan of the ZX-9R B series improvements would be made, but the

A great bike, but the Ninja was a little podgy beside the 'Blade for serious sportsbike freaks. (Tom Critchell)

PR damage was already done. For thousands of potential buyers – irrespective of whether they could actually get the best performance out of the machine – wanted to buy the sportiest machine they could, and the ZX-9R simply wasn't it.

The Ducati, on the other hand, was all it was cracked up to be, and more. Only a few details really kept it behind the Honda. First, even though the 1992 and '94 FireBlade was a pretty uncompromising beast, it wasn't as uncompromising as the Ducati. You virtually *wore* the Duke – it could be a little cramped for taller riders, and those bikers who were carrying a little excess weight could also find it a little hard to get comfortable behind the tank. Ride it through town, and after just a few minutes the 'bum-up-hands-down' feeling would start to make your wrists ache. Sure, the bike wasn't meant to crawl through town, but many bikers would not be traversing gorgeous twisty sections of B road every day.

Also there was the spectre of poor reliability. Hondas were renowned for the fact that they were (and still are) bolted together very well and as a whole are extremely reliable. Even looking at the minimalist FireBlade you could see it had some lovely little touches and an excellent finish that made it difficult to think of it as a mass-produced machine.

The Ducati was drop-dead gorgeous – it was the only machine of the time that made the 'Blade look ordinary. It even looked well put together, and the Bologna firm had made great strides with the reliability of their machines, as they have done to this day. But bikers are an unforgiving bunch with long memories. The thought of 1970's and 1980's Italian electrics and mechanicals may have made many unfairly turn their backs on the machine.

And finally there was the price. At £11,800 the Ducati 916 was £3,605 more than the FireBlade and that meant it was out of reach for many bikers'. Well, all but the most affluent. So, compared to the new kids on the block that year, the FireBlade still reigned supreme.

'Some manufacturers can't even build a 600 that weighs so little. And none of them can build one that looks so gorgeous. Honda are the best production engineers in biking and the quality of even the tiniest brackets and lugs reveals a religious attention to functional beauty.' ***Performance Bikes*, April 1994 – CBR900RR v Triumph Super Three.**

'Think of a sportsbike that displays a total synthesis of design from the front to the back. Engine, chassis, suspension all built specifically and only for the same bike and designed for each other from the start. Chances are you'll think first of a Yamaha and the Genesis philosophy, but it's Honda and their CBR900RR FireBlade who've taken the design to its logical conclusion – the most single-purpose road sportsbike ever built.' ***Fast Bikes*, June 1994 – CBR900RR v Ducati 916 v Honda RVF750 RC45.**

'On the dyno the Honda counters every punch of the 916, then deals a knockout horsepower blow. Two points to the 'Blade and victory by one point. It's faster, more powerful, sharper handling and worth every penny of its price.' ***Motor Cycle News*, 18 May 1994 – CBR900RR v Ducati 916.**

'Just grabbing the CBR's bars and feeling how little resistance they offer to turning gets you in the mood. The light clutch, and slight vibration that comes from a big motor bolted into such a small frame, create a seething expectation of speed and lightness that is immediately confirmed: the CBR lunges forward from 2,500rpm like a mad dog taking its owner for a walk.' ***Performance Bikes*, 1994 – CBR900RR v Kawasaki ZX-9R Ninja v Triumph Super Three.**

'Since its launch in Australia in 1992, the Honda FireBlade has set completely new standards for the opposition to aim at. Any test of pure sportsbikes isn't complete without at least some reference to Honda's instant classic. You hear the name so much, you get fed up with it. Then you ride one on the track and the respect returns.' ***Motor Cycle News*, May 1994.**

'More than ever there's a buzzing, sizzling fire about the 'Blade – even at a standstill. Stubby and chunky, tiny and flighty and a 900, impossibly. The claws of the mighty mouse Honda are now sharper than ever before.' ***Bike*, April 1994 – CBR900RR v Triumph Super Three v Kawasaki ZX-9R Ninja.**

The '95 model FireBlade was still the lion-hearted king of the jungle – especially in the 'Urban Tiger' paint scheme. (*AMCN*)

'First the easy answer. The best sportsbike is the FireBlade. No doubts, no 'ifs or buts', this is the bike that's shaken the class to its roots with its track handling, light weight and storming motor. If you want the ultimate sportsbike it's the only one any serious rider will have on his shopping list.' **Motor Cycle News, 23 February 1994 – Suzuki RF900 v Kawasaki ZX-9R Ninja v Triumph Daytona 900 v CBR900RR.**

'It's not as stable or as torquey in the mid-range as the classy Yamaha FZR1000 EXUP, or as comfortable or rev-hungry up top as the Kawasaki ZX-9R Ninja. But for $15,000 you'll still get the lightest, nimblest big-bore Jap sportsbike going. And that's enough to bring the tiger out in anyone...' **Australian Motorcycle News, 3 June 1994 – CBR900RR first test.**

Aussie MCN veteran Ken Wootton gives it the berries at the Phillip Island launch of the new 1994 FireBlade. (*AMCN*)

'The double-R wins this contest by virtue of what it lacks. Tipping the *Motorcyclist* scales at 457 pounds, the CBR simply lacks weight. 144 pounds fewer than the ZX-11, 114 less than the GSX-R and 76 less than the FZR. Though quirky suspension keeps it a few notches shy of perfection, the CBR900RR remains the purest representation of what a litre class sportsbike should be. It's an amazing sportsbike and for our money the $8,599 price of admission still delivers the best big sportsbike on the planet.' **Motorcyclist, September 1993 – CBR900RR v Suzuki GSX-R1100 v Kawasaki ZX-11/ZZ-R1100 v Yamaha FZR1000EXUP.**

Although the CBR therefore took the honours pretty much across the globe, in group tests it didn't get everything its own way all the time. The new model FireBlade didn't hit the stores in the USA until late 1994 and Motorcyclist felt that the suspension on the earlier model was just a little too harsh for hard use on their roads.

'The CBR is a brilliantly designed, semi-flawed piece of sporting hardware that's too narrowly focused to perform the wide range of duties expected of a modern-day open class superbike. It could be the bargain of the century if you live to strafe apexes all day and can handle the bike's idiosyncrasies. But if you're after a motorcycle that makes your gums sweat every time you flick the garage light on, crack the throttle or throw it into a full-lean left hander the ZX-9R is worth every penny. That's the acid test. And when it's time to go riding, nothing gets us up earlier or keeps us out later than the ZX-9.' **Motorcyclist, June 1994 – CBR900RR v Yamaha FZR1000EXUP v Suzuki GSX-R1100 v Suzuki RF900 v Kawasaki ZX-11 v Honda CBR1000F.**

The 1994 model was finally tested by *Motorcyclist* in their November 1994 issue and was welcomed as a much improved model – by most of the assembled *MC* journalists, anyway.

Jason Black, *Motorcyclist*: 'Last year I picked the CBR900RR as the most potent sportsbike you could throw a leg over. But things have changed since then, I'm a lot pickier about what's good and what's not so good. That happens when you ride bikes such as the Ducati 916, the Yamaha YZF750 and Kawasaki's ZX-9R. In my book the 9R offers a better balance of performance handling and comfort than the RR. Of course, next year I may have to change my mind again.'

John Burns: 'Well aware though I am that the ZX-9R is a far more realistic motorcycle I think I'd have to go with the revamped Honda anyway. I rarely push the thing hard enough to induce any front end twitchiness. If you don't now or never have held a pro racing licence, I doubt it will be a problem for you either. I like

little bikes that don't have much power for sports riding. The CBR has little *and* power, BIG power. Did I mention it makes the ZX-9R look like a recreational vehicle?'

Tim Carruthers: 'Yeah, the ZX-9 probably makes a more tenable street bike and that probably matters… somewhere else. The re-suspended CBR900RR rules these twisty roads …we think. But maybe we'll have to come back tomorrow, just to make sure.'

Mitch Boehm, *Motorcyclist* editor: 'It's no surprise to see Honda try and rid the RR of its collection of suspension gremlins for '95. What is a surprise is that no other manufacturer has come up with a package designed specifically to compete with the RR's serious blend of high power, low mass and nasty boy attitude. After all, the bike sells well in the States and is a full-on best-seller in Europe.'

The opposition were well and truly bloodied and bruised by the 'Blade. In fact, in 1995 1,774 FireBlades were sold in the UK – and that was only a bit less than the sum total of the opposition, which included the 916, ZX-9R, Speed Triple, and RF900.

Honda, though, knew they could not rest on their laurels as the opposition would soon regroup for another assault on the CBR900RR's title of best big-bore sportsbike.

1996 – softly, softly

For the 1996 model year, its first substantial revamp would see the FireBlade moving slowly away from its narrowly focused position as a cutting-edge sportster to becoming more of an all rounder.

Tadao Baba knew in which direction he wanted to take his creation because he'd been listening to the customers who'd bought it.

'We only expected small sales in the first year,' he admits. 'At first we targeted only, say, 5,000 customers a year. So when we thought of the 5,000 riders who would actually buy the FireBlade, we knew they must be very enthusiastic people – and they were focused on what sort of bike they wanted. That's why we could make the bike in the way that these

enthusiastic people preferred. During the first year of production, it suddenly began to sell unexpectedly well. That's when we received more and more feedback from the owners. They would say to us "put a passenger grab rail on the pillion so I can take my friends for a ride", or "please make the pillion seat wider and more comfortable for my girlfriend", or "can you make the windscreen bigger for better protection when I'm riding on motorways, freeways and autobahns?", and "please make the handlebar higher for more comfort". And so on.'

These comments were hard for Baba-san to ignore, but he had also to try to keep true to the original design ethos of the FireBlade.

The 1996 FireBlade. At last, one for the masses and the marketing men who wanted to soften its edge so that more riders would take up its challenge. (Honda UK)

'From all the comments I knew these people loved our 'Blade very much. The bike they seemed to want sounded a little like our CBR1000F, but we couldn't just tell them to buy one because they didn't want a CBR1000F, they wanted a CBR900RR FireBlade and all the performance that comes with that machine. However, if we had bowed to all these suggestions, then the CBR900RR would have no longer been the FireBlade. Looking back now, I think that if we had, then the CBR1100XX Super Blackbird wouldn't have been born.'

As well as customers' comments, the marketing men in Honda could also see this machine moving from a small volume machine to a big seller – if the changes made were the right ones.

Baba-san explains: 'At about the same time, our marketing division came to us and said they wanted to sell the FireBlade to a wider range of riders. We had to fight against these pressures, in order to keep the original concept of the FireBlade. Things are very different when we make a bike for 20,000 people, rather than

the 5,000 people we originally aimed the CBR900 at.'

Baba and his design team wanted to keep the sporty image of the FireBlade – and its RR designation – but open up the performance to a wider audience, thereby pleasing the marketing men. The machine he and his team developed for 1996 was argued by many to be the finest FireBlade – just the right mix of performance, character, and usability. Optimal mass centralisation was still the name of the game, which helped make this later

version of the new RR lighter and more powerful. Keep the bark but lessen the bite is pretty much what they wanted to do.

Power was up to between 123 and 128bhp at the crank thanks to a 0.10 point compression ratio rise, and a significant 1.0mm overbore. The CBR now displaced 918.5cc and featured a host of improvements to the 1994 model (see Chapter 3 for a full run down).

Styling-wise the look of the FireBlade changed a little, with fish gills appearing on the tail unit and the holes disappearing from the

The 1995 and '96 models show their differences. Contrary to popular belief those holes in the fairing actually worked. Well, Honda said so. (*AMCN*)

fairing sides – although the front of the fairing still resembled a Swiss cheese, as did the rider's heel plate. Another nod to lightness.

Originally the holes in the side of the fairing were on the bottom and top. They came about thanks to a fashion in the late 1980s and early 1990s which saw race bikes adopt them big time.

Race-spec NSR250s and NSR500s started to appear on grands prix grids, with people saying that the holes both saved weight and helped the rider turn the bike, due to reduced air resistance. When the works Hondas started turning up on the grid with them in 1990, paddock cynics wondered if you could actually

buy these 'works' or 'factory' holes!

Holes are one thing from the 1990s GP circus that didn't really catch on – unlike aluminium beam frames and inverted front forks. Still, Honda gave it a go, and FireBlade development rider Dave Hancock insists that adding nothing to a bike can, in fact, work.

He recalls: 'I remember looking at the holes in the fairing at the launch of one of the models – they're a trademark of the FireBlade now – and wondered if they would actually work. They were supposed to help the rider turn the bike from one side to another and I reckon they actually did that! On the 1996 model we had a hole in the front fender through which air would rush at speed and this was to give the front wheel a little more control. Again I was sceptical, but during testing we covered the hole up with tape and the bike felt a lot less stable.

'In fact, the earlier "twitchy" front end was helped enormously by that mudguard, making the bike that bit easier to ride. This was one of Baba-san's pride and joys of this model of FireBlade. Without the holes, we found in testing that we were getting downforce, but the holes helped manoeuvrability at high speed. All of these little things worked and helped a great deal and that meant we could develop the 'Blade bit by bit. Again, we'd ridden all the other machines at the time and we were confident that we could beat what was around or coming around.'

While the holes had disappeared at the bottom of the fairing, it was also claimed that the new mudguard actually circulated air under the fairing, helping to support the rider. How? Well, the lower pressure air behind a fairing's bubble usually pulls the rider's neck and head down, leading to shoulder and back strain. Not so with this design, said the designers.

The changes to the 'Blade were mainly this, says Hancock. 'Most important for us was to get power up and weight down while changing the shape of the torque curve to make it more manageable on the road. We deliberately set out to make the bike so much more user friendly.'

Likely the only changes the average CBR900RR owner would have actually noticed were the reworked handlebars, the 10mm (0.4 in) higher seat, and the much narrower, more svelte fuel tank. These improvements combined to give the CBR a much lighter, easier to handle feeling. Previously, the tank would get in the way of knees and elbows when cranking in hard to a turn: Now the tank – which on earlier versions felt as well as looked

Tim Thompson of *Bike* magazine found the '96 CBR was suitable for a much wider audience. (Jason Critchell)

huge – proved not to be such a barrier, making the bike feel smaller because of it.

Power was still there in rich abundance. Bang the throttle up to the 11,000rpm redline and the rider had better be pointed in the right direction.

Tim Thompson from *Bike* magazine admitted that the new seating position could open up the 'Blade to a whole new audience.

'Out goes the wrists down, arse up stretch which puts the CBR off limits to so many shapes and sizes. I prefer the CBR600 – an instantly accessible sportster – get on and go bonkers in seconds without being intimidated or locked into a bizarre riding position. Except now the CBR900 is in every way like its all-round stablemate: easy to ride, comfortable, proven, and very, very quick. If you can afford to run a ten-grand motorcycle, there is now no penalty for cubes.'

Other UK magazines agreed that the best had just got better – as well as that bit more comfortable. *Motor Cycle News*'s Chris Moss said at the launch: 'Honda has worked miracles with its new 1996 CBR900RR FireBlade. Despite targeting the bike at less sports-orientated riders by relaxing the riding position and smoothing out the power, the result is a bike that's an even better out-and-out sports rocketship. It's quicker, better handling and much easier to ride hard. The changes mean you're able to move around the bike a bit more, especially in the corners. And cornering is still what the FireBlade is all about. Some may lament the absence of the old motor's kick at 8,000rpm, but the new motor makes it easier to ride, especially if you want to go fast.'

Richard Fincher, deputy editor of *Ride* magazine, said: 'Hang on? What's all this nice boy bollocks? Aren't 'Blades supposed to be tendon-tweaking, neck-scrunching sports tools, edges rougher than a freshly-sawed plank, with enough twitches to keep a Prozac factory busy for a year? Yet here it is. The FireBlade for 1996 is relevant and relaxing.'

Despite the loss of that head-banging image, after a few laps Fincher found the new bike just as exciting but with a tad more forgiveness. Well, that's what people thought he said.

'Slap this puppy hard and it'll slither away,' he drooled, 'but it takes a measurable moment to get to full trouser-loading effect and there are enough incoming signals to get a bit of rear brake on or wriggle it far enough upright. Forgiveness isn't up to Mother Teresa levels, but it's better.'

Over the pond in the USA they were also finding that while this wolf was disguised, it wasn't so much in sheep's clothing as something a fair bit nastier.

In Australia, Marton Pettendy attended the Down Under launch for *Australian Motorcycle News*. 'It's taken a sportsbike of the calibre of Ducati's svelte 916 to knock the FireBlade from its Best Sportsbike perch over the last two years, though the lightweight 900 has continued to feature highly as an honourable mention in our annual awards. I guess the bottom line is that the two causes for concern on last year's FireBlade have been remedied. For me the CBR9 is now comfortable enough to seriously consider as an everyday streetbike and the plusher, more precise front-end and slightly more compact overall feel only tends to further heighten this new bike's user-friendliness. It's good to see a motorcycle manufacturer listening to what its customers want and in the case of the 1996 FireBlade, the

Sadly 'Urban Tiger' was extinct. In its place for 1996 were these colour schemes. (Gold and Goose)

ergonomic improvements seem to have come without any performance trade-off.'

Aussie MCN's Ken Wootton managed to get in a spot of back-to-back testing on the 1995 and '96 'Blades. Here's what he said: 'Refinement is the key to the new FireBlade and riding the old and new back-to-back has helped amplify those differences. Sure, there's not much been altered at first glance, but the little things add up. The improved reach to the bars, the narrower tank, the more precise front-end.

'Minor the changes may be, but the better steering of the new 'Blade and the loss of that "wooden" feeling makes for a more confidence inspiring ride at full noise.'

Aussie buyers, who found problems distinguishing new CBR600s from old ones had stickers on the machines to help them recognise later ones – and so it was with the latest FireBlade. A sticker saying: 'FireBlade 919 Edition' on the frame told people that this was the 1996 bike and not the similar 1995 model.

Cross the Pacific Ocean and the story was still the same. Andy Saunders from *Motorcyclist* said of the 1996 machine: 'The capabilities of this bike are frustrating at the track. It's one that repays seat time with even greater levels of performance. Or maybe I'm just rusty. Anyway, after many laps around Willow Springs I found myself only just starting to trust the revamped Honda at the end of the day and then even more amazed that it would go wherever I pointed it. Okay Honda, you've convinced me, lighter and more powerful means faster and better.'

Other members of *Motorcyclist*'s crew felt the same. Less is more, but with more comfort it proved to be more still. In the February 1996 issue they said: 'The 1996 double R may look very much like its predecessors, but a few miles in the saddle are all you need to realise that this version is profoundly different. To wit: no more compromises. Not only does the '96 version continue to define the term "crotch rocket", it's now also a relatively nice place to sit and take in the scenery. At the end of the day, what looks a lot like just another CBR900RR has become a completely rehabilitated beast, ready to be let loose in society.'

All the various improvements also seemed to come in for praise from the *Motorcyclist* staff – especially the suspension, which seemed to be a major bug-bear with the Americans on previous models. 'I don't remember this road being so smooth,' they said. 'Whatever Mr Baba and his crew did inside those 45mm fork tubes and remote reservoir shocks it works amazingly well. All we know is that both ends of the CBR do a fantastic job of erasing the bumps at any speed, from zero through hero and well into fear-o.'

And the rest of the staff?

Mitch Boehm: 'Those who worship exclusively at the altar of race track prowess might not agree, but this is clearly a better streetbike than the original. Roomier, more comfortable, more ergonomically correct, better suspended and much easier to ride quickly, the second generation double R is the sport motorcycle Honda engineers were after in the first place. I've heard good things about the new GSX-R750, but it's gonna have to be damn good in lots of areas to beat this thing.'

Kent Kunitsugu: 'Make no mistake, the 900RR is now definitely a far better streetbike. But I wish Honda would swallow a little corporate pride and toss the 16-inch front wheel.' (All Kent had to do was wait a few years for Honda's pride to catch up with itself – see Chapter 8.)

John Burns: 'The RR was already Earth-shattering, now it's gone inter-galactic. Nobody but Honda could have built the original 900RR and nobody's going to build a better four-stroke street bike because lightness is the most expensive thing and nobody has more money than Honda. "Yes, but what about the Ducati V-twin rumble," I hear you say? I'm tired of it, man. This RR will rip a 916's liver out and make some weird Japanese meal out of it.'

With the 916 filling everyone's ultimate wish-list in 1996, it was – perhaps – understandable

Suzuki's new-for-'96 GSX-R750 was hot favourite to take the 'Blade's crown. (Tom Critchell)

that this was the ultimate machine that people had in mind for pitting the new 'Blade against. Although maybe this was a little unfair, considering the huge price differential in all the European and US markets. But still it happened.

Tim Carruthers: 'On paper, the original 900RR was the perfect low-mass, twisty road scalpel. On pavement, jittery, high-speed cornering manners could expand eyeballs and contract sphincters beyond standard tolerances in the same fast bend. Anybody but Honda would have retreated to a 17-inch front wheel and standard steering geometry. But Mr Baba's boys have come up with an RR that smokes the landmark original everywhere. Is it really that good? Let's just say that, unless you enjoy adjusting your desmoquattro valves, there's no logical reason to wait in line for a Ducati 916 anymore.'

But riding it in isolation was one thing, testing it against the latest tackle would be another.

For 1996, Suzuki would launch their new and updated GSX-R750. Here was a bike with more heritage than the FireBlade (the first GSX-R was released in 1985) and claiming almost as much power. What it did have over this new 'softened' FireBlade was attitude. GSX-Rs always seemed to represent the hooligan element of biking society – just the element that flocked to the CBR900 when it was launched in 1992.

Gone was the top-heavy double-cradle frame of old, replaced by an up-to-the-minute aluminium beam frame and an all-new motor. Suzuki said it more than aped Kevin Schwantz's 500 GP championship winning RGV500. Initial reports at track launches were good.

Bike's Phil West said: 'It's low, light and tight where the 1995 FireBlade would feel tall, bulky and incohesive by comparison.'

Okay, so West hadn't ridden the latest FireBlade, but on paper the GSX-R750 looked very good. Wheelbase was 5mm (0.2in) down on the CBR. Weight was 4.5kg (9.9lb) down, and its claimed power-to-weight ratio was 704bhp per tonne to the CBR's 688bhp/tonne.

Another 750 that saw the light of day at almost exactly the same time was the Kawasaki ZX-7R. Derived from the 'Blade's earlier sparring partner, the ZXR750L, the 7R wasn't playing the same game as the GSX-R. It was heavier – 203kg (447.1lb) compared to 179kg (394.3lb) – and basically seemed a more street orientated option.

At the launch at Jerez, many Kawasaki officials were telling any journalist who would listen that they simply wanted to build a road bike that was safe. They still produced a race dedicated RR version, but in standard form the bike just wasn't in the 'Blade and GSX-R league.

Still, it was a handsome devil and it still had a lot of track achievements behind it, thanks to its older ZXR brother.

Eventually *Motor Cycle News* in the UK got both the GSX-R and the FireBlade back-to-back in the cold of Northamptonshire in January 1996.

Both were declared winners.

Chris Moss said: 'From the extremes of sun-baked Continental race tracks to the misery of British roads in winter, everywhere and every time we've ridden these bikes we've been impressed. Choosing which is the best overall is impossible. Both are winners – one on the track, the other on the road. The FireBlade gets the vote as the better road bike, while the GSX-R is a different animal. It snorts and sees red the moment it's fired up. This is the clear focus that has made it the best Japanese sportsbike ever seen.'

One bike that many expected a lot from was the Yamaha Thunderace. Here was a bike, descended from the once-mighty FZR1000EXUP, that had surely come to claim Yamaha's sportsbike crown back?

The specs sheets said that the Yamaha YZF Thunderace wasn't going to pull any punches. At the heart of the 'ace was a 1,002cc inline four-cylinder motor with an output of 130bhp and a dry weight of 198kg (436.1lb). Initial reports were very favourable, with many believing that the Thunderace could, just maybe, have the legs on the Honda CBR900RR FireBlade on the road.

At the launch in South Africa, *Motor Cycle News*'s Moss reckoned the YZF was just excellent on the road. He said: 'The Yamaha has the balance just right. It's not perfect, but the YZF1000 Thunderace's versatility makes it

At a shade under 200kg (440.5lb) and with a 1,002cc motor, the Thunderace was a very fast and very stable road bike. (Yamaha UK)

an astounding road machine. Comfort and ease of use have to be considered for day-to-day use and Yamaha's Thunderace is king of the real-life road.'

It was going to be tough, but Honda personnel were confident they had second guessed the opposition enough to build a bike that could beat what was coming in 1996.

Hancock explains: 'We felt at the time that the torque the FireBlade motor had would beat the 750s, while the machine's light weight would see off the threat of the Yamaha Thunderace.'

The ultimate test in the UK was held by *Motor Cycle News* in March 1996. All the major sportsbikes of the year were assembled at Cadwell Park race circuit in Lincolnshire. The

machines arrayed before *MCN* road-testers Chris Moss and Marc Potter were: Yamaha YZF1000 Thunderace, Kawasaki ZX-9R Ninja, Suzuki GSX-R750, Ducati 916, Kawasaki ZX-7R, and the Honda CBR900RR FireBlade.

In the race to be the boss of the race track, Moss crowned the Suzuki king, saying: 'Suzuki's stunning GSX-R750WT is the most single-minded, frantic road bike money can buy. On the track the lightweight, high-revving racer-like edge makes the bike so satisfying.'

The verdict? 'Suzuki's awe-inspiring GSX-R750 stands out as the clear winner on the track. It's a clearly-focused machine built with one thing in mind – going fast. It's got a combination of blistering 168mph [270kph] top speed and near-perfect handling, along with fearsome brakes, which make it brilliant on the track. The winner of the closely fought battle for second is not so clear. Yamaha's Thunderace lapped very quickly at Cadwell. It's very easy to ride fast thanks to a strong engine which is more forgiving than the Suzuki if you get it wrong. It was a surprise how fast Kawasaki's ZX-9R lapped. The massive potential of that awesome motor is finally unleashed thanks to well-suited Bridgestone BT56 tyres. It was the fastest bike on Cadwell's back straight, which gained it a lot of time on the stopwatch. Ducati's 916 has long been known as an excellent track tool, but at Cadwell it gave way to the superior horsepower of the others. A top-end power deficit and less effective brakes left Honda's FireBlade lagging marginally behind the ZX-9R. It hasn't suddenly become incompetent. It's still very satisfying to ride hard. It's just that the competition has got hotter. Kawasaki's ZX-7R couldn't display its full potential because of unsuited tyres that failed to warm up in the cold. Even so, it was a fraction off the pace. All these machines are utterly brilliant track or road bikes, but the bottom line is lap times. And they clearly show the Suzuki as the winner.'

Shocking though the prospect was of Honda's best finishing third, this test, to be fair, was a dedicated track one, albeit with a veneer of road riding; and it must have been difficult to conduct a reasonably accurate test in the UK in early March, as this time of year isn't the best for testing high-performance motorcycles.

Superbike sent their Bike of the Year bash down to France, but even they seemed to think that the 750s had caught the 'Blade on the track. 'The FireBlade is definitely lacking,' said tester Ian Cobby. 'It's showing its age. The 750s have caught up and overtaken it.'

The people who seemed to matter – the bike-buying public – didn't care what *MCN* or anyone else said. Sometimes the FireBlade won, sometimes it didn't. Whatever happened, overall the edge was still with the CBR. Maybe it was the Honda badge, maybe it was the extra cee cees, maybe it was the years of development. Maybe it was just the name. Thunderace? Pah! FireBlade sounded much cooler. And you could now ride and tour on this super-cool superbike. This practicality was obviously very important.

Proof of the pudding is, as they say, in the purchasing, and still the 'Blade was the best seller in the UK. Ever since the launch back in 1992, sales had grown, and grown. To illustrate: 1992: 1,106, 1993: 1,126, 1994: 1,774, 1995: 1,648, 1996: 2,400, 1997: 2,866.

Enviable, utterly enviable for the opposition. But still they couldn't topple it. Favourable reports and even an advertising war in the UK between Suzuki and Honda, swapping explosive quotes from the *MCN* tests, didn't actually change things.

The Honda CBR900RR FireBlade still sold more. And by now the FireBlade had finally begun to make the large impact it deserved back home in Japan, thanks to the softening of the previously focused CBR, as well as a change in policy.

Satoshi Kogure, of *Young Machine* magazine: 'Since about 1996 the FireBlade's character had grown gentler and gentler by going through its many modifications – although it also ended up losing some of its original purposeful charisma year by year. The enthusiastic hard-core CBR900RR FireBlade fanatics in Japan might have felt sad about that somehow, but I think it was OK because it gradually changed the "not-for-everybody" bike into a "possibly-for-me" bike, taking the top spot in the large sportsbike category. Another reason for its improved sales was that over-400cc bikes suddenly became very popular in Japan, thanks to the big change in the licence system in 1997, and as a result the FireBlade steadily grew more popular. It was still far from being the top selling bike in all categories – like it was in the UK – but it now had the steady popularity that it deserved.'

Respected Japanese freelance journalist Yuko Sugeta put it perfectly in a way only the Japanese could: 'I saw the first model as a deep and narrow well which only a few people could reach the bottom of to get the water. The later model was an even deeper well, but wider, too, so that more people can get the water, but still only a few people can reach the bottom.'

Baba-san knew just why he wanted more people at the well to get the water.

He said, 'Every time we updated our FireBlade, I heard calls from those 5,000 enthusiasts who we originally targeted the

Motor Cycle News's chief road tester Marc Potter on the 1997 model CBR. It still outsold its rivals – a superb 2,866 units in the UK that year alone. Britain, it seemed, loved 'Blades. (*MCN*)

FireBlade at, complaining about the milder performance, even though over the years the performance of subsequent machines was actually better and better. The difference is that many more people can now enjoy the 'Blade, and if some talented, enthusiastic rider tries to push it harder, he or she will see even more performance waiting to be enjoyed. He will see the shining star of the FireBlade. This is the same for all of the later models. It has never lost, and will never lose, that edge. But as you turn pockmarks into the attractions of the bike – for example an uncomfortable bike into a comfortable one – in the eyes of some riders the product loses its edge. Many people started to tell me that the 'Blade was not like the original FireBlade any more. They said it had lost its sharpness. The first one had a strong individuality, and I understood that. Our

work over the years has concentrated on how to make it easy and safe for riders to pull the ultimate performance from the CBR900RR. In fact, the FireBlade has not lost its sharpness. But people feel that it has because it has become easier to ride. This paradox has always been with us.'

By the end of 1997 the opposition were closer than ever, but the Honda CBR900RR FireBlade was still there at the top of the pile. No one manufacturer had beaten Honda because they seemed too scared to actually take the 'Blade on at its own game of mating a lightweight chassis with a high power motor. There was still no production machine capable of opening up a rider's vein and mainlining their adrenaline rush in such large doses as the FireBlade… But the king's reign was about to come to an end.

Owner: Dave Baker. Many rate the 1994-5 Foxeye 'Urban Tiger' colour scheme as the best ever for the FireBlade. (Jason Critchell)

Owning the ultimate

A big plus point to owning a FireBlade is the fact that it is a Honda. Honda's are well known for being incredibly well put together and have an enviable reputation for quality and reliability. Despite the fact that the FireBlade had been built down to a weight and a price it still looked solid and robust, and pretty soon it was found that it performed as good as it looked.

This was demonstrated early on in the CBR's life when, in October 1992, Portuguese magazine *Moto Jornal* and Greek mag *Moto* got together on the demanding Estoril circuit to thrash the living daylights out of a 'Blade for a full day, to see if anything would go wrong.

The bike was a tired press machine which had already had a hard life, both at the hands of journalists and, later, with Honda staff when it was used for homologation testing. A service and a change of brake pads, and the bike was ready for its 24-hour ordeal. *Moto* editor Vassilis Karachalios was on hand to take part and act as scribe for the day.

He recalls: 'We started this test with the sole intention of mercilessly thrashing the FireBlade until it begged for mercy. But it had other ideas. At the end of the test it laughed at us, as if to say "is that all?"

'Here's what happened:
Saturday **12.30pm:** We hope to finish the test in exactly 24-hours – and no sooner because of crashing! I nearly come off exiting the pit-lane when I give the bike too much throttle! Not a good start. Must remember to scrub the tyres in first.
2.20pm: The rear Michelin Hi-Sport is shredded already; we change it.
2.50pm: New rear helps us to highest recorded top speed of the test 166mph (244kmh).
4.00pm: All riders are settling down now and are lapping in the 2m 06s to 2m 10s bracket. Off the bike we can't believe how easy it is to turn the bike into the corners. Even if you're tired, just stick either knee out and the bike simply obliges instantly.
4.45pm: Pit for new front tyre. Lap times immediately fall to 2m 04s.
5.40pm: Quickest lap yet, 2m 02s.
6.35pm: No signs of any problems after six hours. Brake pads changed.
8.25pm: First laps in darkness. The track is full of rabbits! I can't avoid two of them and kill them. One of the mechanics grabs a scooter and retrieves them for tonight's dinner.
9.10pm: More preload and compression damping for the front forks is needed. After so much abuse the oil inside must have turned almost to water. The rear shock was at full compression/rebound/preload right from the start.

One of the biggest thrills in biking in the1990s: throwing your leg over a FireBlade for the first, frightening time…
(John Noble)

11.20pm: Oil check – no noticeable change from before the start almost 12 hours ago.
Midnight: Change of brake pads and a new chain. As we throw the old chain on to the ground it snaps in half! We were lucky that didn't happen in the darkness at full throttle.

Sunday **12.40am:** The rabbits, like the FireBlade, still prefer the racing line. I keep one thumb on the horn, just in case. Our best lap times in the darkness are in the 2m 08 second bracket, which says a lot about the brightness of the FireBlade's headlights and our foolishness.

3.00am: The suspension is terrible now and bumpy turns are becoming a real problem.
6.30am: Another new front tyre. We check the oil again. Still no consumption after 18 hours on the track. Riders change every hour.
10.20am: The rabbits have disappeared now,

leaving behind lots of casualties. Thankfully the 'Blade has proved to be completely rabbit proof. Pit for new rear tyre. With daylight again and despite the awful suspension we and the 'Blade can still cut 2m 02s lap times. That's very impressive.

12.31pm: The ordeal for the FireBlade the riders and the rabbits is over. The bike was still idling after 24 full-throttle hours, without the slightest trace of mechanical noise. The standard suspension did have a hard time, but mechanically the bike is sound – apart from a slightly loose end can. Very impressive. All the riders ranged in height from 1.65 to 1.85 metres and they all found the CBR comfortable for the long stints in the saddle.

All in all we covered 520 laps of the Estoril circuit, totalling 1,540 miles (2,262km). We used 340 litres of fuel at 15 litres per 100km.'

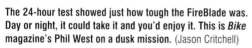

The 24-hour test showed just how tough the FireBlade was. Day or night, it could take it and you'd enjoy it. This is *Bike* magazine's Phil West on a dusk mission. (Jason Critchell)

With years of building specials and GP bikes behind them, the Harris Magnum 5 was always going to be something special. (Roland Brown)

Super-trick CBRs

While the standard machine's performance was astounding, many people felt that they could make big improvements on the original FireBlade.

Some of the world's biggest names in the tuning business have turned their hand to producing better 'Blades. Here's four of the best, as described by Roland Brown.

Harris Magnum 5 (1995)

Like its predecessors stretching all the way back to the Magnum 1 in the late 1970s, the Magnum 5 is an aggressive, hand-built cafe-racer. This bike is the most stylish of the lot, with a neat twin-headlamp fairing, lashings of carbon-fibre, and a 916-style high-level exhaust system. This Magnum's forks are raked at 25°,

compared to the standard 1995 CBR's 24, and its wheelbase is 45mm (1.8in) longer at 1,450mm (57.1in). Overall the seating position is more like that of the 1996-model FireBlade, roomy and comfy. Numerous carbon-fibre parts, including the self-supporting seat unit (the rear section, like most of the fairing, is glass-fibre), means that the Magnum's weight is almost identical to the 185kg (407.5lb) of the standard Honda. Relaxed geometry means that stability is excellent, with the Harris keeping its head on roads that might well have got a standard 'Blade in a bit of a flap at the same speed. Harris brothers Lester and Steve built the bike because they felt that the standard '95 machine was still a little twitchy. And with a number of trashed standard bikes the whole

With an even bigger power-to-weight ratio than the standard machine, wheelies were all too easy on the Roca Overlight.
(Roland Brown)

Magnum kit comes in cheaper than a rebuild. The steel tube ladder frame is a real head turner!

Roca Overlight (1995)

This is a smart FireBlade. A power output of 150bhp is matched by a claimed dry weight of just 152kg (334.8lb), over 30kg (66.1lb) less than the stock donor CBR.

The Overlight's look and its basic layout are close to standard, but almost every component has been revised or replaced in the search for more speed and less weight. Most obvious is the single seat unit, which, like the pair of silencers inside it, is made from carbon-fibre. The fairing combines a standard CBR top half with slatted sides and an aerodynamic lower section of Roca's own design. The standard frame and swingarm are anodised gold to match.

Suspension consists of a pair of very classy upside-down racing units from Dutch firm WP,

complete with hand-adjustable preload knobs on their tops, plus a French-made Fournales air unit at the rear. Wheels are lightweight magnesium three-spokers from an outfit called Dominator, wearing Michelin Hi-Sport radials. The front brake set-up comprises fully-floating 320mm rotors gripped by six-piston ISR calipers, with Kevlar pads. ISR's tiny rear disc has so many holes drilled in it that it's almost invisible, and at just 210g (7.4oz) is a quarter the weight of the standard one. Carbon-fibre is scattered all around the bike, from the front mudguard, via footrest shields and clutch cover, to the tailpiece. Roca says the bike weighed an even lighter 148kg (326lb) with its original carbon fairing, which was replaced when the bike was repainted. Further evidence of fanatical weight-saving is also apparent in the microscopic mirrors, the drilled front mudguard stays and foot-controls, the scores

For a bike without the originals' sporting pretensions, the MotoBlade handled superbly. (Roland Brown)

of lightweight bolts, the repositioned aluminium battery box, and even the narrow-gauge drive chain intended for a 500cc GP bike.

Some serious work has gone into making the engine suitably powerful. Its capacity remains at 893cc, but compression ratio is up from 11:1 to 12:1, and the motor contains hot cams, 1.5mm oversize exhaust valves, and a lightened and balanced crank. Breathing in through a set of 39mm Keihin smoothbore racing carbs, and out through a high-level, four-into-one-into-two Fulgur Racing exhaust system. It kicks out a whopping 150bhp at about 11,000rpm.

It also has some history behind it, having been used to win a 1,000km (621-mile) endurance race at Circuit Carole, outside Paris. With 150 horses pushing a similar number of kilos, the Overlight has a power-to-weight ratio approaching that of a World Superbike factory racer.

Piot Moto FireBlade (1993)

The name might be a bit long-winded but the bike is short and blunt, looking purposeful in a way that few unfaired machines approach. In place of the CBR's twin-headlamp fairing and low clip-ons sits a big round single headlamp, a simple pair of chrome-plated clocks and a set of slightly raised handlebars bolted to a shiny milled alloy top yoke.

With the fairing removed, the thick alloy frame spars are obscured only by carbon-fibre shields. More carbon is visible in the tank, the single seat, the footrest shields, and the rear mudguard. A pair of upside-down forks hold a 17-inch wheel and a pair of four-piston Brembo brake calipers. Bright red engine cases match the finish of the bodywork. The rest of the angled-forward motor is largely obscured by the radiator and surrounding plastic, by thick braided oil and

Peeking under the fairing of this standard-looking Mr Turbo CBR is like looking at a stripped-to-the-waist heavyweight before the big fight weigh-in. (Roland Brown)

coolant hose, and by the matt-black downpipes of a Devil four-into-one exhaust system, which ends in a big brown carbon can on the bike's right side.

The visual effect is striking because you don't expect to see Honda's fearsome FireBlade with its internals hanging out for inspection. Piot's bike is like a retro-bike with balls (an impression that must have been even stronger with the spoked wheels that were originally fitted). This bike would doubtless be good for a genuine 150mph (241kph) despite aerodynamics like the Eiger's north face, but there's no way you'd keep it up for long. And it goes around corners, too. Front suspension is a hefty pair of multi-adjustable race-spec Kayaba forks, with a race-spec Showa at the rear.

If you had to compare this to anything it's like a smoother, much faster (if less torquey and soulful) four-cylinder version of Ducati's 900 Monster.

Mr Turbo Honda CBR900RR (1995)

This Honda CBR900RR's bodywork is totally standard, with just a few stickers covering the unchanged black, red, and silver paint scheme. It wears stock suspension, original-equipment Bridgestone tyres, even the boring old standard silencer.

But this is one of the most powerful FireBlades on the planet. Look more closely, and you notice the boost gauge tucked discreetly into the left fairing upper, and the small fuel/air ratio gauge with its row of coloured lights bolted on below the speedo. There's a strange little box on the rear mudguard, too, which looks suspiciously like part of a water-injection system, fitted to keep a highly tuned motor in one piece.

But peek inside that oh-so-deceptively standard fairing and you can just make out the four black downpipes converging at a

The Erion Racing road 'Blade looks more like a CBR with just a paint-job, but this is one of the most heavily developed FireBlades ever. (Roland Brown)

particularly compact Rayjay turbocharger which gives this 'Blade a 180bhp kick. The only major strengthening necessary for this CBR lump to handle the turbo was to its clutch, which was fitted with stiffer EBC springs and beadblasted steel plates.

And for those who are really serious about horsepower, there is always the option of taking things a stage further by turning the boost right up to around 12psi – which is 220–230bhp! Madness!

Erion Racing FireBlade (1993)

If any modified 'Blade would feel sharp it would be this one, because Erion Racing's machine is a street-legal version of one of the fastest CBR900RRs ever in America. In 1993 an Erion Racing CBR900RR, ridden by Larry Pegram and journalist Nick Ienatsch, took the open class endurance series, and this is its road-going offspring.

It's a real monster of a motorcycle: a highly tuned, titanium-kitted 931cc rocketship that produces 170 rear-wheel horses at 11,500rpm, wears some seriously trick cycle parts and weighs just 155kg (341.4lb) wet. It was clocked at 177mph (285kph) on the straight at Elkhart Lake racetrack, and hits 145mph (233kph) at the end of a standing quarter.

At first glance it looks like any other 900RR with a pipe and a paint job, but look closer and the clues are there – partly in non-standard cycle parts and the single seat with its champion's No1 plate; more so in the fairing scoop that ducts air via aluminium tubes to the Honda's pressurised airbox. From there it's a short run to the carburettors, which are a set of 39mm Keihin FCR flat-slides identical to those of the race bike. HRC pistons 1mm oversize increase the CBR's capacity from 893cc to 918, at the same time raising compression slightly to 11.3:1. The ported and polished cylinder head contains stock valves, titanium retainers, and Erion's own race-profile cams. Conrods are also titanium, bolted to a polished and balanced crankshaft. Erion Racing's own four-into-one pipe completes a package that delivers a rear-wheel maximum of 144bhp at 10,800rpm, a very healthy 30 per cent up on the standard bike's 113bhp on the same dyno.

The Honda's stock frame holds milled-from-solid Erion yokes, which grip a pair of RC45 upside-down fork legs. These are 41mm in diameter, multi-adjustable, and reworked by Erion to be slightly softer initially, and slightly firmer towards the end of their travel. The front wheel grows in diameter from 16 to 17in. Both wheels are lightweight Marchesini, the rear a whopping 6.25-inch wide item that wears a 190/50-section Bridgestone developed for the RC45. Brakes are standard FireBlade. Rear shock is from American firm Fox, and like the forks is multi-adjustable. Other bits that catch the careful eye are the RC30 footpegs, the twin headlights from a CBR250RR, and the big curved radiator from an RS250 racebike.

Home-made 'Blades

With between 40,000 and 50,000 FireBlades having been sold around the world, it's little wonder that while the big tuning houses have sold tens of thousands of tuning bits for 'Blades, as many owners are desperate to put their own touch of individuality on their CBR900RR.

Performance Bikes magazine got together 50 owners of Honda's masterpiece to find out what goodies and bits and pieces they'd bolted on to their pride and joy. Here's four of the best.

Owner: Mick Higgs

Mick's managed to get plenty of power from the motor, thanks to a fair bit of work. The bike's looks are enhanced by the Harris single-seat tail unit with under-seat exhausts leaving that lovely RC30 single-sided swingarm and RC45 rear wheel exposed. Top speed: 164mph (264kph); Max power: 127.8bhp; Engine: 944cc Wiseco big-bore kit, skimmed and gas-flowed head, Barnett Kevlar clutch, one-off exhaust system from MHP, 39mm Keihin flat-slide carburettors; Chassis: Stock 1992 FireBlade frame; Race specification Kayaba inverted front forks, Fox rear shock, Brembo 320mm discs and four-piston calipers; Yoshimura yokes from solid billet, Honda RC30 swingarm and RC45 rear wheel and all-new tail unit. (Jason Critchell)

Owner: Richard Spencer

While it may not be that fast or that powerful compared to some trick 'Blades – due to only mildly modded engine internals – Richard Spencer's FireBlade is a unique piece of machinery. It's a hybrid, spawned from the FireBlade, Ducati 916, and Triumph T509. It fits Richard's bill perfectly – it looks superb. Top speed: 156mph (251kph); Max power: 119.8bhp; Engine: 1996 CBR900RR-T motor, standard airbox, K&N Filter, Dynojet kit, Skorpion (Akrapovic) header pipes with Remus end cans; Chassis: Spondon frame, single-sided swingarm and fuel tank; Triumph T509 front-end (clip-ons, Brembo wheels front and rear), top yoke and rear hub. The subframe, tail-unit, and nose cone come from a 916. Strangely, it has a Kawasaki ZXR750 sidestand. It also features an Ohlins rear shock and a bar-operated rear brake. (Jason Critchell)

Owner: Mark Reeves

This bike looks like a refugee from the World Endurance Championships. Like Richard, Mark hasn't gone for much in the way of engine modifications. Instead he's gone for some beautifully attractive race track looks, with a single-headlight and Honda Japan lookalike colour scheme. He turned the bike into a special after flipping the standard bike while wheelying outside a McDonalds!
Top speed: 155mph (249kph); Max power: 116.5bhp; Engine: 1992 CBR900RR-N motor, K&N air filter, Dynojet kit, MHP twin under-seat carbon-fibre end cans; Chassis: Kayaba front forks, modified sub-frame, DBR rear-set footpegs and sprocket cover, 320mm Ferodo front disc kit, Yoshimura yokes, RC30 swingarm, RC45 hub, wheel and caliper. Stock 1994–5 Foxeye fairing, filled-in for endurance one-light look. Single CBR400RR headlight, covered by part of an iridium visor. Harris tail unit. (Jason Critchell)

Owner: Dave Baker

Many rate the 1994–5 Foxeye 'Urban Tiger' colour scheme as the best ever for the FireBlade and that is why Dave has kept his. Another splash of retina-shattering orange is courtesy of the exposed rear wheel on the VFR750 single-sided Pro-arm. Even with a pretty standard motor, the visuals make this a gloriously aggressive streetbike. Top speed: 163mph (262kph); Max power: 119.1bhp; Engine: Standard 1994–5, but with Dynojet kit, K&N air filter and full stainless steel under-seat Harris exhaust with carbon fibre end cans; Chassis: VFR swingarm braced by Martek, VFR wheel and hub, Harris Magnum 5 subframe and single seat tail unit. (Jason Critchell)

Celebrity FireBlades

With the CBR900RR's reputation for affordable speed, agility, and outright performance, it's understandable that a few famous names would end up having one in the garage.

Phillip McCallen – 11 times Isle of Man TT winner and FireBlade development rider
Despite being in on the whole CBR900RR FireBlade project from 1991, it wasn't until 1993 that Phillip finally got his hands on the bike he helped develop.

'Finally, when I eventually got hold of one I knew just what I wanted to do to it to make it work just a little bit better. The two things I wasn't a big fan of on the original 'Blade were the sensitive front end and the brakes, so I got the front end from an RC45 along with the yokes and replaced the entire FireBlade assembly. The yokes allowed a 30mm (1.2in) offset, which with a 17-inch front wheel and a slightly longer frame allowed me to have the same wheelbase but with the advantage of good, low profile 17-inch rubber. I always thought that the use of a higher-profile 16-inch tyre could lead to excessive tyre flex, and a few years later – at the 1996 Production TT – it was proved in a picture that was taken of me in the race. You could see the front tyre deforming – scary! The brakes I swapped for a six-piston set-up with bigger discs for more braking performance and better feel. Some of my ideas were incorporated into the later FireBlades. The best model in my mind was the 1998 FireBlade, but by then the bike had been caught up – if only in performance terms – by Yamaha's impressive YZF-R1. It's amazing to think that it's taken them six years to catch up with the 'Blade and even then the 1998–9 model is still there or thereabouts.'

Despite developing the FireBlade, Phil waited a few years before taking the plunge and buying one. The result was a bike that would help in the development of later machines. (David Goldman)

It looks a mess, but it barks – just like the owner! Keith Flint and his FireBlade that matches his on-stage persona. (Jason Critchell)

Keith Flint – the frontman with The Prodigy

It looks well used, but that's a good thing. Keith Flint – whose hit records include 'Firestarter' and 'Breathe' – isn't your standard pop musician who gets on board with the latest fads, such as bikes, just for the sake of his image. He's a handy rider and racer who believes that handsome is as handsome does. That's why this FireBlade is not the best looking in the business.

He's spent quite a few years developing his FireBlade and has spent around £28,000 on the bike.

'I think a bike should go well before it looks good. And this performs really well. I've had the speedo off the clocks and then some. We got 171.3mph [275.6kph] out of it along the Bruntingthorpe runway one time on different gearing than standard.'

The specification of Keith's FireBlade is impressive. Inside the motor is a 972cc big-

bore kit with JE Pistons and a gas-flowed big valve head. The engine breathes through 39mm Keihin flat-slide carbs without filters on them. Jetting is swapped from standard to a Dynojet kit for optimum jetting. The bike has a full-system Skorpion exhaust and a Dyna 2000 ignition box.

All this adds up to a very impressive 152.8bhp on the dyno at 11,000rpm. A beefed-up clutch helps control the power and the wheelies. Keith says: 'I don't do very long wheelies. Just a bit of first and second, really. I'm not really keen on them – I used to do them outside the youth club when I was younger, but got sick of watching my bike banana-ing down the road after falling off so I don't do them very much now.'

To keep the power on the road the chassis features re-valved front suspension, and an Ohlins rear-shock. Braking is from AP Racing six-pot calipers and AP Racing discs on PVM six-spoke magnesium racing wheels. Keith also has Yoshimura rear-sets on the bike for a sportier riding position. Plain white aftermarket bodywork replaces the Repsol-Honda replica crash-damaged original – told you he rides it hard.

'At the end of the day I simply love my FireBlade,' he says.

Mark Knopfler – musician, singer with Dire Straits

He's got a seriously exotic collection of cars at his West London home – including a Maserati 300S from 1956 – but Mark Knopfler loves bikes.

He started out on two-wheels when he adopted a derelict, engineless Triumph as a lad. His stable of two-wheeled machines now includes a Honda VFR800I, which he uses for everyday transport; a Vincent 'B' Rapide (which he prefers over the faster Black Shadow); a 1998-specification Sanyo Honda CBR600 racer which was taken to second in the 1998 British

Sultan of Swing: Knopfler and his racing íBlade. (Honda UK)

Supersport 600 Championship by Steve Plater; and a Sanyo Honda FireBlade which was raced by Paul 'Marra' Brown in the 1997 British Production Series.

Mark – whose time with supergroup Dire Straits in the 1970s and '80s resulted in many hit records including 'Sultans of Swing' and 'Money For Nothing' – uses both the Sanyo bikes for track days, whenever he gets the chance. And he loves the FireBlade.

Money-raising vicar Paul swapped 'fire and brimstone' for 'FireBlade and Bridgestone' and raised £20,000. (Nick O'Brien)

'My best biking moment must be going around Goodwood during an exclusive track day. I was going far too fast following Sanyo Honda rider Steve Plater and team boss Mick Grant. Russell Savory, who tunes all the bikes, was there as well, and he doesn't hang about, either.'

He's keen on spending more time on the track whenever he can. He says: 'It's my ambition to get faster and smoother on the track with Mick and co. But I've no plans to go wheelying down the entire length of the pit straight while doing so like Plater! It's too late for me to go racing bikes. I've started way too late, but I love biking, bikes, and my 'Blade.'

Reverend Paul Sinclair – celebrity vicar and fundraiser

'My FireBlade is worth almost £20,000 to me. It's not the tuning bits, the Zebra paint-job or even sentimental value that dictates this price. It's because with the help of my FireBlade I've raised over £19,000 to buy a bookmakers next door to my church and turn it into a youth centre. I realised the traditional biblical "fire and brimstone" approach wasn't going to work so I decided to get on my bike and use "FireBlade and Bridgestone" to get the results.

'With that wondrous 16-inch front wheel, brakes to die for, and the bike's hooligan reputation, my FireBlade was just the tool I needed to win over Joe Public.'

With all the media attention, Paul gained sponsorship from a number of leading motorcycle accessory firms. The 'Faster Pastor' appeared in the bike press, national and local press and radio, and even national TV. The money continued to pour in, but as the stunts became more outrageous in a bid to get more publicity, it did lead to a little accident.

'While practising stoppies I slid forward into the tank at speed and, well, more than one lump came to my throat. The bike leant itself to

publicity with its easy wheelie nature, knee down dynamics and general good looks.'

The Revvin' Reverend's 1994 'Blade came in the classic 'Urban Tiger' colours of rich metallic gunmetal with orange tiger stripes, but this scheme was perhaps a little too aggressive for a man of the cloth. So top UK paint shop Dream Machine sprayed it black and white – to make the world's only 'Urban Zebra' 'Blade. Horse power was replaced by Zebra power.

'With the bike as the star I found myself writing monthly articles for *Bike*, and other magazines around the world as well. Each and every article was copied and sent to the directors of William Hill – who owned the bookmakers – with a quote from Jacob in Genesis: "I will not let you go until you bless me." It worked, as eventually the chairman himself sent me a cheque for £100 to cover my costs with the words: "Bless You!" Finally we were able to take over the bookies and start work on converting it into a youth centre – most of this thanks to my FireBlade.

'My CBR900RR is truly for the fundamentalist preacher. It's Fun, Damned good and just a little bit Mentalist, too.' Amen!

Around the world by 'Blade

Circumnavigating the globe is a serious undertaking and one that is much better suited to a full-on touring bike rather than a FireBlade. But two people have completed such a feat on Honda's best-selling sportsbike – Jeremy Pascoe and Sjark Lucassen. Here are their stories.

Jeremy's story

'Go around the world on a FireBlade? Why not? I couldn't tell you what actually prompted me to do it. Sure, the choice of bike was a little unusual, but it was easy. The FireBlade was – and still is, even after my 70,000-mile adventure – the best affordable performance bike I've ever ridden. So the idea of selling it to buy something sensible for the big trip didn't even come up. What's sensible, anyway? All I can say is that, at the time, it seemed like the right thing to do. When I'd decided to do it, bit by bit the planning for the trip began to come together. Chance encounters with people who knew people who could help became the norm. To give my trip a real reason, I decided to contact the Macmillan Fund for Cancer Relief, a charity my family had become involved with the year before and whose excellent work I had seen at first hand. I pledged to ride 40,000 miles on their behalf and a publicity campaign was formed. People called, unexpectedly, and offered their help. Camping equipment, clothing, helmets, tyres, even an airline contributed. In return, my once-standard red, white, and blue 'Blade was plastered with logos and turned into a visual poke in the eye.

'Of course, there were setbacks. An air freight company tried to rip me off three weeks before I left, but again, it all worked out. Mike Allen a fellow traveller put me in touch with Virgin; Virgin put me in touch with Air New Zealand. Problem solved!

'Potential problems with the bike were of little concern. Why should they be otherwise? It's a Honda FireBlade! As long as you lube the chain, check the tyres, change the oil, etc, every few thousand miles, why should it go wrong? It wasn't as if I was going off road (or

Jeremy and his 'Blade on their travels. (Turn One)

Top ten tuning tips

If ever one man understood FireBlades, other than project leader Tadao Baba, then it would be Phillip McCallen. The Ulsterman has developed the 'Blade and won TTs on it, so he knows how to make one really hustle. He now runs the Motorcycle City race shop in the West Country. Here's his top ten tips for a better 'Blade.

1: End-can

Many modern slip-on cans no longer need re-jetting to suit them, so for just a small outlay you can add a little individuality to your bike. You can get two varieties. Road legal or race. Road legal will make less power (if any – it's not unheard of for slip-ons to make *less*) and less noise. It will also have a BSI mark somewhere on it. Race cans will give you a much better sound and around 1–2bhp. Some may also have 'not for road use' on them somewhere, making it easy for the police to nab you. Systems that work well with all models of FireBlade include Micron, Remus, and Yoshimura.

2: Dynojet kit

Modern motorcycles in the UK are tested for noise and emissions at around 5,000 revs, so many machines suffer from a 'flat-spot' in this area in which the bike takes a dip in power to keep both emissions and sound down. This comes in just when you don't need it on the road, so it's beneficial to get rid of it. Fiddling with the jets in the standard carbs can make a difference, but the best way to recalibrate the carbs is by fitting a new jetting kit – Dynojet is the most popular. This fills in the hole, makes the bike more responsive at lower revs, and can add a brake horsepower at the top-end.

3: K&N filter

The key to more power and more top speed is making the bike breathe better. In Stage One terms, this is a case of an end-can or full system, re-jetting, and fitting a freer-flowing air filter. Simple to fit, these are guaranteed for life.

4: Full exhaust system

Exhaust systems that have tailor-made headers/downpipes and end-cans should work better together and offer less resistance to escaping exhaust gases. Generally for sportsbikes like the FireBlade these will be non-road legal, full race-systems, costing anything up to four times that of an end-can. Matched with a filter and calibrated with a jetting kit, you can get another 10–20bhp – although some race systems will push the power higher up the rev range at the expense of mid-range grunt. Popular makes include Akrapovic (previously Skorpion), Yoshimura, Micron, Hindle, Remus, Two Brothers Racing, Erion Racing, and D&D.

5: Sticky tyres

It makes sense to keep your pride and joy on the road. The first thing in contact with the tarmac is your rubber – so make sure your tyres are the right pressure and the right compound for the job that *you* demand of them. Early in the FireBlade's life it was hard to get anything other than the standard Bridgestone Battlaxes, but nowadays many different makes and compounds are available. Evaluate your riding. If you do a lot of track days then the sportier tyres could be for you; if road riding is all you do, stick with tyres recommended for the road. Some race tyres will have sharp profiles which make it easier to turn into corners on a track, but are an unstable wobbly liability on the road.

Popular tyres for the 'Blade include Bridgestone Battlax BT56 and BT56SS, Dunlop D207, Michelin Pilot Sport, Pirelli Dragon Evos, and Avon Azaros.

6: Steering damper

Keeping your bike steady at speed is important. Many FireBlade riders are in two minds as to whether a steering damper is actually needed – but many prefer the secure feeling of damped-down steering – and anyway, they look the business. Popular makes include Ohlins, Maxton, and Harris.

---

so I thought) and I'd already arranged to get the bike serviced by Honda when necessary.

'The surprise of the trip was that time and time again a casual conversation over a cup of coffee would alter the direction of my trip, or at least the route I had planned.

'For example, the couple I met en route out of New York who put me up in Texas a month later. And a Japanese biker in Mexico put me in touch with his friends in Japan who were planning to ride around Australia on 50cc Honda scooters. A wrong turn in California led me to meet up with a group of canyon racers who go by the name of the Squid Hunters. They serviced my bike and organised a track day at Laguna Seca. I also met ex-Grand Prix champ Barry Sheene in Australia after a chance encounter with his neighbour's son up a

A bewildering array of bits is available for any model of FireBlade.

7: 17-inch front wheel

The 16-inch front wheel was a compromise for the FireBlade. It was needed to help keep the weight of the bike down and make it steer quickly. But this also had two negative aspects. First, it meant that it could be a bit of a handful over bumpy roads if you really had the skill to *use* the performance; and secondly, the lack of sticky rubber available for the high-profile 16-incher. Many may find the 16-inch set-up works for them. That's fine – comfort and confidence on a bike is subjective. But most race FireBlades have switched to a 17-inch front set-up, as has the latest Y2K FireBlade. Swapping the front for a late model CBR600 front wheel works with the minimum of fuss.

8: Adjust/re-valve forks and rear shock

We're all different. Riders' sizes range from tiny jockeys to big Sumo wrestlers – and we all want to enjoy the most performance from our bikes. It's therefore common sense that standard suspension set-up won't work for everyone. If you can't go to a specialist race service centre to get your suspension tuned to your riding and weight, then experiment. Make small adjustments, a little at a time and ride familiar roads to see if it's an improvement. Make sure you note down the changes so you can put the bike back to standard if it doesn't work or if you sell the bike. If your FireBlade has a hard life it can pay to have the fork internals re-valved, by fitting different weights of spring and oil – again this may suit the

rider's weight. On older model 'Blades, replacement shocks can help performance, as well as the looks of the bike. Suspension tuners in the UK include Maxton, Hagon, and Dave Parkinson, while popular shocks include Ohlins, Maxton, Hagon, Fox, Tech2000, and Penske.

9: Gas-flowing/blueprinting

Remember what we said earlier about making an engine breathe better? This is the next stage. Gas-flowing is where the engine surfaces in the top-end of the motor are smoothed out so that the fuel and air mixture can flow evenly into the cylinders. You can get power gains of up to 5 per cent on standard. And blueprinting? This is a big job. It involves taking every engine component and machining it to the exact manufacturer's specification. This removes the inaccuracies introduced by mass-production. It's best to go to well-known and respected tuners for this sort of job, such as Tony Scott, PDQ, RS Performance or TTS.

10: Big-bore kits

These can either be a dream or a nightmare. You're increasing the capacity of the FireBlade motor from 900cc (on the older 'Blades) to close to 1,000cc on later models. Piston kits include JE, Cosworth, and Wiseco. Again, go to the best tuners to avoid cowboy bodge-jobs which can leave you with holes in your bank balance and sump.

mountain near Brisbane, 200 miles away. Got lost in Melbourne and stumbled into the "Cafe Racer" in St Kilder – the most hospitable cafe I've been to anywhere. They fed and watered me, put me up, provided support and back-up throughout my stay in Oz and took me to not one but two track days at Phillip Island and to the Melbourne F1 grand prix circuit. The most wonderful single group of people I have ever

met, and one I shall return to see again. They also serve the best coffee in Australia.

'The list of odd events, coincidences, chance encounters, goes on and on. But one thing is for sure: without them it would have been a long holiday. With them it was an adventure. So, what did I learn from the trip? How to keep an open mind for a start. To give people a chance, to trust in strangers. I learned self-reliance, and that when given a choice, I chose to do the right thing, regardless of personal cost.

'And the bike? Well, it's now done a total of 83,000 miles, and has a cracked fairing courtesy of a kangaroo in Western Australia – not too bad, considering we came together at about 140mph! I broke three fingers, dislocated my left shoulder, and cracked my left knee. The 'roo didn't make it.

'But travelling for any period of time is about several things: the places you go, the people you meet, and the things you learn. And there is a lot to learn. I read somewhere once that it's not the destination that's important, it's the journey. How true. By the time I came home the FireBlade was something so special to me. It had shared my adventure and now it sits in pride of place in my front room!'

Jeremy's trip facts

Countries: 17; Continents: 3; Miles (on trip): 68,795 (110,691km); Total FireBlade miles: 83,000 (133,547km); Sets of tyres: 10; Clutches: 3; Clutch cables: 3; Chain and sprocket sets: 5; Brake pads (sets): 5; Full services: 12; Lubed chain: 311 times; Adjusted chain: every 2 days; Head race bearing (sets): 1; Exhaust end cans: 2; Rear shocks: 1; Valve clearance adjustments: 3; Accidents: 3; Collisions with kangaroos: 1; Robbed at gunpoint: 1; Speeding tickets: 0 (!!!!); Longest day: 1,487 miles (2,392km).

Sjark's story

With its huge aluminium 'snail shell' secured in place of the pillion perch and rear tail unit, Sjark Lucassen's FireBlade must have been a strange sight during its 110,000-mile (176,990km) trip.

It all started in May 1995 when the potato farming Dutchman set off from his home in Maashees in Holland with his 50,000-mile-old FireBlade on a trip of a lifetime. From then until 1999, when he finally arrived back home, this remarkable man had the most incredible adventures.

As well as the massive 20kg aluminium 'thingumy' on the back of the bike, Sjark also fitted a Scottoiler, a K&N Filter kit, a steering damper (important on some of the very rough roads he found himself on) and Fuelstar, which is an additive which allows the use of some of the lower octane fuels found in other parts of the world.

Of all the places that he visited, Sjark remembers Russia most fondly. 'The people there are extremely friendly. It's unreal. They are totally different from what I believed about them. People would wave me down on the side of the road and offer me food and vodka. I swear I was 10 kilos heavier when I left.'

During his time in eastern Russia he was even held up in his tent by four men with knives who wanted money. 'They asked me for dollars and I told them I had none. We talked for a few hours, and by the time they left I think they were ready to give *me* money.'

He also had two crashes in Russia – although both were down to parking in soft bitumen with the sidestand digging in. The worst road was also in Russia, where a waterlogged bog meant it took him 10 minutes to move just 100m.

When he reached Japan and the Honda factory, they were so impressed with his efforts and the condition of the bike that three white-overalled technicians took the bike away and gave the machine a full and free overhaul

Sjark on the road. (Sjark Lucassen)

Top ten buying tips

1: As with any bike the golden rule is history. Don't always go for the youngest machine, as a year-old bike with a hard life from a hooligan rider will not be such a good prospect as a three-year-old one with less miles – especially if owned by a perfectionist who keeps it immaculate. Always be on the look-out for people with six-month-old bikes who've scared themselves silly and just want rid of it. Bargains like these are there to be had.

2: Although not many FireBlades have been raced, some may have found their way on to the track. Telltale signs are: lockwired sump plugs and immaculate bodywork on a tatty bike – racers will use pattern bodywork, so the original stuff will be hardly used.

3: Always try to buy standard. You know all that tuning stuff we've just talked about? Yeah, great, but to buy a perfect 'Blade (or more importantly to sell one) try to keep it standard. If you're buying, just look for something as clean and straight as you can. If you're selling, either bolt the standard bits back on and sell the trick bits separately or offer the original bits to the buyer to sweeten the deal. A bike with an end-can and Dynojet kit are acceptable, but get the standard silencer for later MOTs. Also, if you want a tuned bike, find out who did the tuning – are they reputable?

4: Always run a line down the bike to make sure it's straight. FireBlades are for experienced riders only, but we all get it wrong occasionally, so a plank of wood down the side of the bike tyre-to-tyre will give you a good idea if everything's true or not.

5: With crash damage in mind, remember that aftermarket paint jobs may point to a tumble – especially on aftermarket panels/fairings. Also, these cost a fortune to replace. Use scratches as a haggling point.

6: Haggle like mad if the bike you want to buy has shot chain/sprockets or tyres. Big-bore sportsbikes like the FireBlade can be hard on these consumables, so budget for these and haggle accordingly if they need replacing.

7: We said history is important – so ring HPI to check if the bike has been stolen or written off or has finance outstanding against it. What price peace of mind? The same as three tanks of fuel! You can call them on 01722 422422 – or check number with local police station.

8: Go prepared. If you don't know the average price of the year of FireBlade you're looking at, then you are the one at a disadvantage. Prepare by reading *Motor Cycle News*'s Bike Mart, *Ride* magazine's Bike Hunter, and scouring the local papers' ads to gen up on prices. If you know someone in the trade, beg or borrow *Glass's Guide* or the *CAP Green Book*. These are the traders' bibles when it comes to buying or selling. Forewarned is forearmed!

9: In the UK there are two markets operating side by side. Official bikes from the importers, and parallel bikes, ie those that come from other markets in Europe or further afield. These aren't dangerous bikes, but generally dealers will pay less for them – and so should you. Giveaways of parallel imported machines are headlights that dip to the right and not the left, kph speedos, and headlights that stay on all the time. Some are well disguised, so if there's any doubt take the frame and chassis numbers and ring the UK importers. They'll know.

10: Golden rule: don't buy a stolen bike. If the frame and engine numbers don't match, then walk away. Numbers that look tampered with are a similar giveaway.

---

including the replacement of brake pads, calipers, and discs – all free of charge.

Sjark has many stories from his adventure. Like the time he had to use an inner tube in his tyre as the tubeless one was so shot (even the inner had 11 patches and a 2-inch gash sewn up on it). Or the times in Bangladesh when, in areas marked out of bounds to tourists, he would have to whizz past the checkpoints at speed – completely illegally.

Despite being miles from home; 'on Monday mornings I'd find that I wouldn't be missing home at all,' he says. 'There's nothing I'd rather be doing than riding.'

Sjark's trip facts
Countries: 40; Continents: 4; Total miles: 100,231 (161,402km); Tyres (front): 11; Tyres (rear): 19; Punctures: 25; Chain and sprocket sets: 3; Fuel: 8,500l (1,870gal).

The ultimate challenge...

'My childhood dream was to be a champion of motor racing with a machine built by myself' – *Soichiro Honda*

For a machine that wasn't the right capacity for the more popular of production racing classes, the Honda CBR900RR FireBlade has finally matured into a respected adversary on tracks around the globe.

The initial problem for the 893cc machine was that few classes actually catered for it. Generally the major four-stroke categories that dominated world class national and international events in 1992 were the 400cc, 600cc, and the 750cc Superbike class. But in some places – notably the USA – large capacity production race classes still existed, and it was here that the fearsome-looking Two Brothers Racing CBR900RR took the FireBlade's 'power to the people' and 'light is right' concepts to their almost illogical race extremes.

Two Brothers Racing was formed back in 1987 by brothers Kevin and Craig Erion. Their close links with Honda meant that they were allowed to get hold of an early 1992 CBR900RR and begin to work their magic on it. Kevin recalls: 'That first 900 responded beautifully to our modifications. Within a week of getting the bike we gained some serious horsepower and lost a lot of weight.'

Modifications to the motor included just an exhaust pipe and carb jetting swap. The Two Brothers Racing jetting kit retained the stock airbox of the '92 CBR and offered a variety of main-jet sizes along with different needles and slide springs. Initially only a Stage One kit was developed using the existing airbox and filter, but later a Stage Three kit was fabricated along with individual air filters over the carbs.

The TBR CBR barked through a gorgeous small-bore, four-into-two-into-one nickel plated steel exhaust system which had an aluminium end-can. Even these small modifications on this early bike hiked power by 12bhp, from 118 to an impressive 130bhp at the rear wheel.

Almost more impressively, TBR had managed to take the anorexic 'Blade's weight down even further. In 1992, *Motorcyclist* magazine got the TBR 'Blade on the scales, and found that with a full tank of petrol it weighed in at 191kg (420.7lb), while the road machine with a full tank weighed in at 208kg (458.1lb).

'We saved about 15lb [6.8kg] with that first exhaust pipe alone,' recalls Kevin, 'and we were confident that we could save more with later, stainless steel systems. We saved a further 18lb [8.2kg] on new bodywork. We also made a set of lightweight clip-ons for the rider

The 1993 Unlimited Team Challenge-winning race bike. The race fairing hid numerous changes. (Roland Brown)

and lost more weight by cleaning up the tail section and scrapping the pillion foot pegs, turn signals, and other non-essentials. The weight was quite a bit lower – and that was despite adding a steering damper and a larger front wheel.'

Road CBR900s had the (in)famous 16-inch front wheel, which bestowed a legendary turning capability to the FireBlade in road trim, but in mid-1992 trying to find decent race rubber to fit the 16-incher was difficult to say the least. That's why Two Brothers Racing adopted a 17-inch front wheel from a Honda RC30. This gave TBR a much wider choice in proven, race-winning rubber.

Despite more suitable, stickier race tyres coming on stream in later years in the 16-inch size, TBR, and later the Erion championship-winning machines, always stuck with the 17-inch set-up – one later copied by the Honda factory themselves for their 2000 model FireBlade.

Just swapping the front wheel over was a problem. Nothing that American Honda had would simply bolt in. Finally, TBR went with a European-specification RC30 front wheel and machined a spacer to mount the CBR900RR discs. The stock calipers could then mount in their normal position.

The bike – impressive as it was – was never

raced in 1992. Instead it was developed ready for the 1993 GTO Endurance series.

In its first year it was impressive, winning five from 11 starts with Kevin Erion as team captain and crew chief. Unfortunately, at the end of 1993 Craig and Kevin went their own ways following an acrimonious split. Craig stayed with Two Brothers Racing, while Kevin went off to form his own company – Erion Racing. Following the split, Erion dominated in the large capacity production class. Since it began racing the CBR900RR in 1994 it has won the championship every year bar one (1995). Even a cursory look at the results makes amazing reading.

Results with race prepped CBR900RR

1993: Kevin Erion team captain and crew chief. The team won five out of 11 races to win the GTO Endurance series.

1994: Again the Erion 'Blade won five from 11 races to win the newly named Unlimited Team Challenge.

1995: Third overall. First place went to the factory entry from Suzuki, who won the Superteams series.

1996: Three first and four second place finishes out of nine races during the season.

1997: Won seven out of nine rounds of the renamed Formula Xtreme series. Finished both first and second overall in the series.

1998: Won 10 out of the 11 races. Again finished first and second in the series.

1999: Total domination. Won every race in the series to again finish first and second.

Some big names in USA racing have raced and won on Erion Racing CBRs. Kiwi racer Andrew Stroud secured a brace of titles, Kurtis Roberts (son of 'King' Kenny) won the 1999 championship, while other riders have included the likes of Larry Pegram, Tripp Nobles, Mike Barnes, Doug Toland, Nick Inatech, Eric Bostrom (brother of 1998 AMA Superbike champ Ben), and Nicky Hayden (from the trio of racing Hayden brothers.)

In recent years the survival of the Unlimited/Xtreme series has been in doubt because of a lack of support from some manufacturers, but the competition has improved the racing breed for Erion. The totally dominant 1999 Erion Racing CBR900RR has moved the game on, just like the road bikes did.

A look at the specifications for Kurtis Roberts' championship-winning machine shows just how far the bike has come in Two Brothers' and Erion Racing's hands.

The 1999 Erion Racing Formula Xtreme CBR900RR is a far cry from many race 'Blades around the world which have to adhere to more stringent production rules, but it is a work of art which also goes very fast indeed.

If you could actually look inside the motor you would find many parts developed by Erion or sourced directly from Honda's specialist race division, HRC.

The cylinder head has extensive head and porting modifications to ensure optimum ingestion, combustion, and exhaust of fuel/air and exhaust gases. Erion-developed race-only cams move the race-only titanium valves up and down, also on modified springs and valve spring retainers. Valve seats have been altered by adding copper beryllium seat inserts to allow the use of the titanium valves. And the combustion chamber was also modified. Erion teamed up with respected engineering firm JE to manufacture specialist race pistons for the bike, bringing together added strength and reduced weight. Pankl titanium con rods are used, as is a modified stock CBR900RR crankshaft. The motor breathes through a bank of Keihin 39mm FCR flat-slide racing carbs and an Erion Racing-developed ram-air system which helps boost power at speed by forcing pressurised air into the airbox and carbs. The

More beautiful with its clothes off than on. The 1999 Erion Racing CBR900RR kicks out a more than healthy 180-plus bhp at the back wheel. This is, perhaps, the ultimate expression of the FireBlade. (Kevin Wing)

stock ignition system is modified from standard with different timing and rev limit to Erion Racing specifications. As if this isn't enough, many of the various moving parts are comprehensively given new finishes and coatings to reduce friction and increase efficiency throughout the rev range. To aid efficient cooling, a modified radiator from an RS250 two-stroke GP machine is used. The result is a claimed maximum power 'in excess of 180bhp' at the rear wheel and a redline as high as a dizzy 13,000rpm. Incredible when you think that the standard

bike manages around 125bhp and a max redline of just 11,000rpm.

To get all that power down efficiently, the standard gearbox and its road ratios were ditched in favour of a HRC close-ratio transmission, with ratios interchangeable for each of the different tracks on the Formula Xtreme calendar.

Another HRC item, a back torque limiting clutch, is also used. More commonly called a 'slipper clutch' in other parts of the world, this enables rapid downchanges through the gearbox without the rear wheel locking up. Useful if you go down one gear too many and you don't want to end up in the gravel trap on your behind.

To keep all the extra stresses and strains of a race-tuned motor in check, the chassis is similarly beefed-up to keep the surplus 'oomph' under control. The frame receives extra bracing in a number of areas: 'We do all the frame bracing at our workshop and we don't like to tell our competitors exactly where,' says Kevin. As well as more bracing on the swingarm to keep all that 180bhp on the track as best as possible, the sub frame was modified to sacrifice more weight. New rear-set footrest hangers, triple clamp yokes, clip-on handlebars, and a hand-made aluminium fuel tank manufactured by Erion Racing, were also fitted, again saving many kilos. Other Erion parts include fairing and instrument brackets and a new battery box.

Suspension is the finest that money can buy. Swedish suspension experts Ohlins – a byword for quality in the race paddock – supplied the front forks, the steering damper, and the rear shock, all of which offer full adjustment in every regime to enable the Erion Racing team to set up the suspension for any track surface.

The standard brakes are ditched in favour of top-of-the-range Brembo Goldline brakes, discs, pads, and master cylinders front and rear. Lightweight Italian-made Marchesini race wheels are used as a replacement for the much heavier road items, while drive to the rear wheel is handled by AFAM sprockets through a DID chain. The whole package is wrapped in Erion Racing Sharkskinz bodywork.

But what's it like to ride this machine, which could lay claim to being the ultimate expression of the whole FireBlade ethos? Mitch Boehm, editor of respected US publication *Motorcyclist*, got the chance to find out after Erion Racing clinched the 1999 Formula Xtreme title. Here's what he said after riding both the 900 and the championship winning CBR600F4 at Willow Springs circuit:

'Kurtis Roberts' championship-winning CBR900RR racer did not feel slow, especially through turns eight and nine, which seemed to melt into one long, horrifying bad trip of a right-hander. I remember frantically mouthing something like "where's the damn short straight? There ain't no short straight here anymore," in my helmet. One hundred and eighty horses coupled to race slicks will do that to a race track, I guess.

'Despite the hyperspace-like rush the thing generated in Willow's fast sections, the 900 was easier to ride than I'd expected – at least at the speeds of which I was capable. First, it was roomier than the CBR600F4, Roberts' larger proportions resulting in an ergonomic set-up more accepting of my own (6ft tall 220lb). It also steered with a bit less effort than the F4 (I'm not sure why), and offered an even more controlled ride, the obvious result of the high-end-and-high-dollar Ohlins fork and shock fitted.

'The long-stroke motor was reasonably flexible, too, making useable power from six grand on up and offering a choice of gears in most corners. Above nine grand, though, things got a bit more interesting, and though I revved the motor into the red zone (12,000rpm) on the straights, I was plenty judicious on the corner exits, short shifting whenever possible. I mentioned this to Roberts later on in the pits, thinking he'd consider me clever for discovering some secret to the bike's success. But he just said, "Nah, ya gotta rev it or else the chassis winds up…" So much for being clever. 'The rest of the package was as slick and trick

Mitch on the Erion CBR. (Kevin Wing)

as you'd expect a Formula Xtreme championship winner to be. Everything from the killer brakes to the trick clutch and electric shifter worked smoothly and harmoniously, and it was obvious the Erion 900RR had years of development behind it. Its limits seemed totally unreachable; even when I got somewhat comfortable with the power and tried to make the thing sweat a bit, it seemed to yawn and

say: "Jeez, Mitch, can't you do any better than that?"

'In the end, even with all that horsepower and Superbike-like chassis performance, I went only a second or so quicker around Willow than I had on Nicky Hayden's 600. Which reinforced that traditional old saw – talent is much more important than power.

'Lesson learned. Again.'

John Burns on working with the Erion 'Blade

'While it lacks the star power of the Superbike class, Formula Xtreme really lets tuners strut their stuff. Reinforcing the frame to contain 180bhp is the first order of business, and that consists of welding extra material in place at the steering head, adding an extra cross-brace up front (right below the stock one), and "boxing in" the side plates.

'In the continual quest to get the RR to exit corners in an orderly fashion, the team has three different rear suspension linkages to choose from: a stock-ratio piece, a linkage with roughly half the rising rate of the stocker, and one in between. The transporter carries four Ohlins rear shocks of differing specification. With limited practice time, it's more efficient to simply swap shocks than to fool around with different settings. (For the record, what wound up working best was the half-stock rising rate, heavyish compression damping and lightish rebound.)

'There are spare fork assemblies as well. If one doesn't work, mechanic Rick Hobbs can say, "let's try the B damping," for instance, and on the fresh new fork goes. It doesn't hurt that Ohlins shaman Stig Pettersson (Pettersson Pro Suspension) is right down the street from Erion in Anaheim, California.

'Beneath the hand-hammered, low-profile aluminium fuel tank resides a 945cc (3mm bigger bore) lump producing somewhere in the neighbourhood of 180bhp. Pankl titanium connecting rods carry JE forged pistons which compress each incoming charge at a 14.25:1 ratio. Big titanium valves are bumped open by cams of Erion design, and the key to how the whole bike works is contained within its bank of 39mm Keihin flat-slide carburettors; if that much power comes in any way other than smoothly when the throttle's twisted, it can be disastrous. Hobbs wound up making his own jet needles and customised the slides, stuck in lighter return springs, and fine-tuned the Keihins' accelerator pumps so nicely that it's actually hard to tell how fast this dang bike really is until it's time to slow down. From way low, there's just a big, deep reservoir of power that makes the bike's RC30 close-ratio gearbox redundant (although its slipper clutch is welcome in all braking zones).

'Must be hard on tyres, huh, Rick?

'"That entirely depends on the rider," Hobbs says. "There's enough power to spin the tyre all the way out of the corner, but one of the first things they learn is less throttle equals faster lap times. It's maybe not as much fun, but that's the faster way." And that's with the rev limiter cutting out the sparks before the old long-stroke RR even gets to its power peak.

'Anyway, it was fast enough to fend off the R1s and carry Kurtis Roberts to three Formula Xtreme wins on the way to his first championship. (Nicky won the other seven, but unfortunately suffered three mechanical DNFs.)

'Things will be different next year. Now that they've tamed the 900RR beast, the all-new, short-stroke, fuel-injected 929RR will carry Erion's riders in 2000–01. No more jet needles. Now it's going to be bytes and chips and laptops. Time marches on.'

Despite the massive success of the older models of the CBR, Kevin Erion says he's looking forward to getting his hands on the 930cc model. 'All we've had a chance to do is take a peek at the new one,' he says, 'but already we at Erion Racing are sure it will provide the basis for a much better race bike.'

The competition have been warned!

The Isle of Man – the ultimate road test, the final challenge

'I here avow my intention that I will participate in the TT race and I proclaim with my fellow employees that I will pour all my energy and creative powers into winning.' – *Soichiro Honda, March 1954*

Back in the United Kingdom at the time of the CBR900RR FireBlade's launch, 1992 saw big-bore production racing pretty much dead in the water. A tragedy at the 1989 1,300cc Production TT race on the demanding Isle of Man TT had done that, as two extremely popular racers, Phill Mellor and Steve Henshaw, died on the same lap in two separate incidents just nine miles apart. The fallout was to see production racing buried both on roads and short circuits in the UK for the foreseeable future.

On a day now known as 'Black Wednesday', tragedy had struck on the second lap of the 1300 race when Mellor's Suzuki GSX-R1100 crashed at the 110mph (177kph) Doran's Bend, and both he and the machine hit the wall. He died later in hospital.

Meanwhile, Mellor's team-mate, future British champion and World Superbike star Jamie Whitham, had crashed at the notorious Quarry Bends, while Henshaw and Mike Seward collided as they tried to avoid the crash debris. Henshaw was killed instantly and Seward was badly injured.

Both accidents highlighted the fact that the big, powerful, unwieldy machines of the day on the tyres of the time were a handful on short circuits, let alone the most demanding road course in the world, where mistakes or even a wobble can lead the rider to make the ultimate sacrifice.

So it took the next seven years for road-based machinery – and in particular suspension and tyre technology – to advance enough for the organisers of the TT to consider letting production machines, especially those in the 1,000cc class, to once again thunder around the 37.73-mile (60.1km) course.

One man who was pushing for the reintroduction of the class was Honda UK boss Bob McMillan. McMillan was a powerful figure at the TT, especially because as far as factory works machinery was concerned only Honda ever really showed up to play at the TT. Bob had an axe he wanted to grind at the TT. Well, maybe not an axe, more of a 'Blade, because he and other top Honda personnel were upset that in Europe the FireBlade hadn't had an opportunity to prove itself the best bike on the world's race tracks.

McMillan and other supporters of the production race badgered the TT organisers until at last, in late 1995, it was announced that four-stroke machines of 701–1,010cc would be allowed to complete in the new Production Race for the 1996 Isle of Man TT.

Honda had the best big-bore sportsbike and it was the best seller. Now they could finally prove it against every other manufacturers' machines.

First and foremost in everyone's mind was to ensure that there was no repeat of Black Wednesday, so the rules were kept simple, but kept safe. Well, as safe as racing the Isle of Man circuit *can* get.

Previously, production rules meant almost no changes at all to the bikes, but for the new proddie class turning the road bikes into

Flexible friend. Phillip McCallen: 'I thought that the high-profile 16-inch tyre would flex around the TT course – and this picture proves it!' (Double Red)

something approaching a 'safe' set-up was allowed.

On the chassis front, rear shock absorbers could be changed, as could all fork internals. Racers could also fit a steering damper – a must at the TT! In the motor, carburettors had to be standard but jetting could be altered, while the airbox and air cleaner had to be as supplied by the manufacturer. The exhaust's silencer could also be changed. Tyres also had to be 'production', meaning street legal and available over the counter. All in all, it resulted in a trickle more engine performance, but a lot more chassis performance, which meant the rules erred heavily on the side of safety.

Good as it was 'out of the box', the FireBlade had to be prepared for the TT races, because after he'd pushed for the race's return for so long McMillan and Honda did not want egg on their faces by losing. This race meant a lot to Honda. Both in the past and now it was important for all the right reasons: it was the ultimate test ride on real roads, and the paying public would see which machine was *really* the best on the road.

For the FireBlade to be ready for the harshest test of all meant testing it on a number of short circuits. Once again, the expert services of Dave Hancock and Phillip McCallen were called in.

Dave recalls: 'I remember just before the TT production race we were testing all sorts of forks and suspension set-ups at Brands Hatch in preparation for the bumps that the Island would throw at us. We tried so many things in the rules, changing to heavier springs, thicker oil and the like, but they were all pretty bad, to be honest. We finally found that the best thing was a brand new set of the standard forks. For that sort of road surface you couldn't really beat the standard forks.'

With McCallen on board – the man most likely to take the late great Joey Dunlop's title of 'king of

the mountain', and with a string of TT wins behind him – it looked like a foregone conclusion, but Honda weren't taking any chances.

A total of 23 of the 53 entrants were mounted on CBR900RR FireBlades, many of them supported through Honda's dealer network. The main competition came in the form of 11 Yamaha Thunderaces, seven Suzuki GSX-R750s (which would fight similar capacity machines in its 'class'), three Kawasaki ZX7-RRs, and two of the bulky ZX-9R Ninjas. Quietly, some TT experts were looking at Yamaha's Thunderace as possibly the machine to watch in the Production Race. Sure, the 'Blade seemed the nimbler of the two and the Yamaha was heavier and longer. But while this may not be an advantage on a short circuit, on the bumpy Island it could lead to a more 'planted' ride, while the extra 100cc could help down the long Sulby Straight and the blast down the mountain. Many Honda riders actually used suspension set-up to lengthen the wheelbase of the FireBlades in order to gain a little more stability.

Added to the fact that seasoned Island campaigners such as Tim Leech, Nigel 'Cap' Davies, and the late Lee Pullan were riding on the Thunderace, it meant that ruling out the mighty Yamaha would be foolish.

Kawasaki's ZX-9R wasn't really in it, with very few riders plumping for the big Ninja, although both cumbersome 9Rs did steal top honours for fastest proddie bikes through *Performance Bike* magazine's speed trap at around 170mph (273kph). In fact the Yamahas came next, and even the GSX-R750s, meaning the 'Blades might even have trouble getting past the smaller machines.

Practice week was hit by the weather, meaning that it was hard to get an accurate picture of the class. FireBlades did fill five of the first seven places on the leaderboard, but surprisingly it was a Yamaha – one belonging

to Dennis Winterbottom – which led the practice times, with McCallen some 2.4 seconds behind.

Despite the threat from the Yamahas and his fellow Honda riders, McCallen – who was heading into race morning looking to complete the hat-trick of his four wins that week – was definitely hot favourite.

But for the FireBlade, three laps of the course – with a pit stop for fuel at some point – could have been its undoing. There were worries in the Honda camp that the 'Blade might not be able to do the two-lap flying stint that would be necessary. A splash and dash in between every lap would be completely out of the question, as such a tactic would lose them any advantage they could gain.

Dave Hancock remembers just who came up with the solution for this one. 'We were worried that at racing pace and racing consumption the 'Blade's 18-litre tank couldn't cope with doing two fast laps of the 37.73-mile circuit. Baba shared our concerns. He simply asked us what the lap length was, how many laps the race was and worked it out himself. He had all the relevant information on specific fuel consumption for this, that and the other jet sizes in his head. He just went up to a blackboard and worked it out. It was remarkable to watch. It showed he knew the bike inside and out. At the end of it all he simply said, "It's OK, the bike will do two laps," and, of course, it did. All he needed was a cup of coffee, a cigarette, an ashtray and something to write down his calculations on. For this reason I'm pleased that Honda have kept Baba on the same project, because on some machines – such as the RC30 and RC45 – you may have two different project leaders, and of course the boss of the later project has to learn the lessons from the first one. Not so with Baba-san. He's lived and breathed 'Blades for more than ten years. This is just one example of how one man working on one project has really helped us.'

So, everything was ready. And as the start numbers were called out and the relevant bikes rolled forward, Hancock watched McCallen's Motorcycle City-liveried number 12 machine roll forward ready for the off.

'Watching Phillip just before the start of that production race, I could see that he wanted to win it for Honda, Baba-san and me as much as for himself,' he says. 'I think as he was part of the test programme he wanted to prove that this bike was the best machine in the world on the harshest road track in the world.'
And prove it he did.

The FireBlades of McCallen and Scot Iain Duffus started the race as they meant to, battling and battling hard. On the opening lap Duffus held a 3.6-second advantage over McCallen, with Davies on the Yamaha a further 3.6 seconds down the road. Fourth at the end of the opening lap was CBR-mounted Colin Gable – who sadly was to lose his life at the TT the following year – with Leech and Pullan close behind.

Second time around both Duffus and McCallen lapped at more than 118mph (190kph) – but Phillip was just faster with an average of 118.93mph (191.3kph). By the end of that second lap the roles were reversed, with McCallen holding a 3.1-second advantage over Duffus, with Pullan, Davies, Alan Bennallick ('Blade), and Nick Jefferies ('Blade) following. Leech retired at the end of that lap, with Gable dropping to ninth.

At the end of the third lap, McCallen came over the line to take the win – his third of race week – watched by an assembled multitude of Honda Japan and UK staff, including Baba-san himself. He'd completed the three laps and 113.19-mile (182.1km) distance with a race average of 117.32mph (188.77kph) – a new record, and one to be expected considering the long layoff for production racing.

Just 6.1 seconds back was Duffus, with Davies in third. Following close behind were Gable, Pullan, and Honda's Derek Young, which rounded out the top six, with Jefferies eventually finishing seventh, just ahead of Bennallick.

Baba's help proved vital. Leaning off the bike a little meant that McCallen could make it home when several riders had run out of fuel. Even Davies had to nurse his Yamaha home.

Honda had proved its point – it was the ultimate test ride for the FireBlade, and it had succeeded.

FireBlades first and second with McCallen (12) and Duffus
(15). 'Cap' Davies (17) was third on the big Yamaha.
(Double Red)

McCallen: 'For me, the picture that sums it all up from that first race was a great shot taken by Double Red photographic. I'd always told Baba-san and the engineers that because a 16-inch front wheel has a higher profile, you'd probably get some sort of tyre flex when you were really on it. I saw the shot in *Motor Cycle News* and you can clearly see the front tyre deforming to keep on the road as the bike's trying to push wide. You can see I was trying hard!'

The following year's race proved to be another win for the FireBlade – and Phillip McCallen – although this time pushing him hard in the controversial race was Scotsman Ian Simpson on a production Ducati 996SPS.

Poor weather saw the original three laps cut

to just two, and this race would prove to be a struggle for both riders. The Scotsman had led from the Ulsterman up until Glen Helen on the first lap, and then McCallen used all his knowledge of both course and machine to reverse this into an 11.5-second lead at the end of the first lap. Simpson wasn't finished, though, and he clawed his way back to finish just 7.6 seconds behind at the flag.

For McCallen, it was a wonder he finished at all, as he'd had a scary moment on the first lap.

'I landed with the steering a bit out of line at Ballaugh, I think it was,' he recalls, 'and that fired me almost over the top of the bike, and the landing twisted the forks in the yokes. From then on I raced with the steering twisted to one side to compensate for the twisted forks and

After a scary incident in the '97 TT, McCallen had to guess whether his steering was straight over the jumps. He still won, despite a dispute. (Double Red)

whenever the front wheel came up or I hit a jump I had to guess if the front wheel was in line. Otherwise I would have been tank-slapped off the bike.

'Despite this problem, in one lap between Glen Helen and Ramsey I was able to make up the gap between me and the leader, Simpson, and take the win. Again, I had to go for the win and prove the 'Blade was the best.'

Following the race, there was an inquiry into whether the fuel McCallen's Motorcycle City-backed bike was using was legal. In the rules it states that the fuel must be pump unleaded available in garages, but the fuel they were using was of a higher RON rating than normal pump unleaded and apparently only available

from one service station – the one situated in the middle of Silverstone race circuit! Race officials threw the protest out and that was that – prompting Ducati UK importer Hoss Elm and Reve Red Bull team boss Ben Atkins to vow never to return to the Island to race.

Overall, again, it was an excellent result for Honda with 'Blades taking seven of the top 13 finishes.

The following year – 1998 – saw the biggest threat to the FireBlade's dominance yet. The all-new Yamaha YZF-R1 had already begun to show its mettle in the showrooms and now it threatened on the roads of the Isle of Man too. Snapping at its heels was also a new, sleeker version of Kawasaki's ZX-9R Ninja. The

How close can you get? 'Hairy' Howarth breathes in and hangs on in the '97 Proddie TT. (Double Red)

spectators relished the prospect of a big fight.

Practice showed that the new, improved FireBlade was in for a struggle. The highest placed 'Blade was that of Michael Rutter down, in a lowly (for a 'Blade) seventh place. At the front Alan Bennallick's R1 just had the edge on Nigel Davies's ZX-9R. To really rub it in, talented Kiwi rider Shaun Harris had sneaked his GSX-R750 ahead of the Hondas too. One place lower than Rutter was Island veteran Jim Moodie, who'd yet to show his hand on the FireBlade. As it was, the race was to be another victory for the FireBlade – and a memorable one at that, as it proved to be Honda's 100th TT win (overleaf).

By 1999 the pressure was beginning to tell on Honda UK, who wanted to keep the FireBlade at the top in production racing in the UK and on the Island. The idea to produce an ultra-trick exotic limited edition FireBlade to run in production racing had backfired, so regular 'stock' CBR900RR FireBlades were to line up against Kawasaki ZX-9Rs and Yamaha YZF-R1s for 1999. Despite the amazing Moodie scooping the win in the previous year's production race, the writing was on the wall. In 1998 Nigel 'Cap' Davies was second (albeit a distant one) on the improved Kawasaki ZX-9R, and relative novice David Jefferies turned in a fine fourth on the R1.

For the final TT races of the millennium, new rules meant that ultra-trick big four strokes

Jim Moodie 100th Honda TT winner

Jim celebrates on the podium with Honda's 1998 president Nobuhiko Kawamoto. (Double Red)

Jim Moodie had never ridden a FireBlade before TT fortnight in the 1999 Isle of Man races, but he still ended up coming home with another FireBlade production race win and – more importantly for Honda – the marque's 100th Isle of Man win.

Moodie had ridden pretty much everything else on the Island: grand prix bikes, big singles, RC45s, Kawasaki ZXR750s, and Suzuki GSX-R750s, but never the mighty FireBlade.

He was ecstatic to get the win – watched as it was by Honda top brass, including Soichiro Honda's widow. 'I was so pleased to be the rider who got the 100th win for Honda on the Island,' he said, 'especially when you think of the greats who rode for them in past years.'

On his second lap he also picked up the lap record for the class, taking the FireBlade round in 18m 45.3s – a lap of 120.70mph (194.21kph). It shattered the old record of 19m 02.2s and 118.93mph (191.36kph), which was set by McCallen in the reinstated

Production race two years previously. It was a dominant win, with Moodie leading every one of the three laps and winning by a margin of almost 30 seconds.

Baba-san was again delighted, especially in view of the competition that year, in the form of Yamaha's R1 and Kawasaki's ZX-9R. 'We are all very pleased,' he said. 'There was a lot of strong competition that year from Kawasaki and Yamaha.'

Nigel 'Cap' Davies (so known thanks to the flat cap that only leaves his head when his helmet is put on) took second on his Kawasaki ZX-9R, Michael Rutter was third on a FireBlade, and David Jefferies came fourth on a Yamaha YZF-R1. For Jefferies, the result in only his second TT was to be a foretaste of what was to come the following year.

Big Jim Moodie in full flight on the Island on his way to an historic win. (Double Red)

such as the Yamaha YZF-R1, Honda's FireBlade, and Kawasaki's ZX-9R could join GP bikes such as the twin-cylinder Honda NSR500V in both the Senior and Formula 1 classes.

Despite the diverse machines that Honda had at its disposal, including the grand prix two-strokes, the V4 RC45, and the FireBlade inline-four, the 1999 event was a whitewash of the most embarrassing proportions for the big H. The Yamaha YZF-R1 not only cleaned up in the production race, but it also won the Formula 1 and the Senior – all at the hands of the relatively inexperienced David Jefferies.

Honda always made sure of harbouring road-specialist talent. Honda UK had specialised in spotting up-and-coming road racers and plonking them on a Honda before they'd had a chance to argue, but it seemed that this particular year they'd missed Jefferies.

It was also sweet revenge for respected Manchester-based tuners V&M, who'd been dropped as the factory team running Honda RVF RC45s in the British Superbike championship the year before. After being dropped they'd courted Yamaha, turned the road-based R1 into an extremely rapid race machine, and taken the rising star Jefferies – nephew of 1993 F1 winner Nick – with them.

Jefferies's contribution to the wins shouldn't be discounted. The R1 was unbeatable that year (R1s filled the Production podium with Welshman Jason Griffiths and Phillip McCallen – the first FireBlade home in the production race came in fourth, ridden by the up-and-coming Adrian Archibald), but he still had to ride it home. Experience at the TT is everything and many feel that you need years of racing at the TT before you have even a chance of a win.

Yet here was Jefferies – who'd debuted in 1996 before missing the '97 TT and proving his ability with fourth in the proddie in 1998 – winning three races in a week, ahead of such experienced Island old hands as Iain Duffus, Jim Moodie, Joey Dunlop, Griffiths, and (an admittedly injured) McCallen.

Jim Moodie in anger – quite literally – on the RS Performance Formula 1 FireBlade at the Isle of Man TT, 2000. (Double Red)

It must have been especially hard for Honda UK to take. Honda prides itself on its TT record over all other race series (surprisingly even the increasingly important and high-profile *Motor Cycle News*-sponsored British Superbike Series) and yet here was more than a bloody nose – it was a knockout victory for the Yamaha YZF-R1.

One thing is certain. Honda Britain consider the Isle of Man to be their very own, and Honda Japan, HRC, Honda UK, and Bob McMillan would be working hard to ensure the trophies come back their way. The sleeping giant was awake for the year 2000 Isle of Man races…

But controversy surrounded the FireBlade's use in the 2000 Isle of Man TT. Joey Dunlop – who sadly died just weeks after notching up his 24th, 25th and 26th TT victories that year – refused to race a Formula 1 FireBlade, which

was developed jointly by RS Performance and Honda Europe R&D.

Instead, the Ulsterman used a VTR1000 SP-1 with a works World Superbike engine from Aaron Slight's machine to take the Formula 1 race. In this race, Jim Moodie took the much-modified F1 'Blade to fifth. He refused to race the bike in the Senior, saying he wanted to ride a machine capable of winning. The fall-out led to Moodie and Honda Britain agreeing to part company, as well as the threat of imminent legal action.

In the rain-hit and much-postponed Production TT it was left to the Yamaha YZF-R1 and David Jefferies to again take the honours. Still, in the hands of *Bike* magazine road-tester Martin Child, a stock FireBlade – armed only with a steering damper – took 30th place in the F1 race. No mean feat!

Short circuit proddie racing

A benefit from the resurrection of production racing at the Isle of Man was the welcome return of big-bore roadbikes to the short circuits of the UK. In 1996 the International TT Production Challenge was really an extension of the proddie TT race, to give the men and machines that beat up the 37.73-mile mountain course a few more outings to make the expenditure worthwhile.

The title went to the wire, with David Jefferies eventually taking his FireBlade to top spot. Second was Jim Moodie on a Sega-sponsored Suzuki GSX-R750 with the same 106 points as Jefferies, a countback of results seeing Jefferies sneak the title win. The sheer number of FireBlades on the grid enabled Honda to win the manufacturers' award that season.

In 1997 the Bike Trader British Production Powerbike Championship was dominated by the booming Ducati 916SPS of TT winner and ex-British Superbike champ Ian Simpson. The Scot took the title for the Reve Red Bull team, beating the Suzuki GSX-R750 of Moodie (again the bridesmaid) into second place. First 'Blade home was Michael Rutter in third place.

The following year saw two proddie series run side-by-side. The *Superbike Magazine* National Sports Production Championship rules meant that the basic rules of production racing (and therefore lowers costs) were kept. This series was won by *Performance Bikes*'s road tester Gus Scott on the new Yamaha YZF-R1, with many of the top runners choosing the advantages of the close-to-stock Yamaha over the FireBlade.

In that year's British Powerbike Championship it was a very different story. The looser rules, along with the tuning talents of Russell Savory, meant that the 'Blade was the one to beat. Add the talents of Sanyo-Honda's Steve Plater and Paul 'Marra' Brown and you had an almost unbeatable combination. Plater took the championship with Brown second.

Dave Hancock was impressed with the machine: 'We dynoed Plater's 1998 series winning bike and found it was pumping out an impressive 154bhp at the crankshaft. That's some serious power and shows how flexible the standard power plant was and how much development was still left in it.'

A return to just one series was seen in 1999 – the

The ultimate short circuit UK FireBlade – Steve Plater's 1998 Powerbike winner. (Jason Critchell)

British Sports Production Championship – and this time Yamaha were dominant, with the top three finishers – Mick Corrigan, Pete Graves, and David Jefferies – all running the YZF-R1.

While short circuit performance of the FireBlade wasn't dominant, as it had been on the roads, there were still a lot of things about the near-standard machine that impressed.

Hancock: 'I remember Iain Duffus at a Powerbike meeting at Donington Park in '97. He was mucking about with the suspension and dropping the forks so far down through the yokes you could hardly see the top of the fork legs above the top yoke. He was still complaining that he just couldn't get the thing to handle around the circuit. I just told him to put everything back to standard. He was a bit suspicious at first but soon was lapping faster than he'd done before. Again that shows just how good the standard equipment and settings were.'

The Production classes still haven't won the hearts and minds of the race-going public quite like the Superbike and Super-sports 600 classes in the UK. The patchy development of rules, regulations, and titles means the class hasn't had the continuity that it needs. In some ways it echoes the Formula Xtreme class in the USA, where manufacturer support is patchy. But few can argue that riders nailing the throttle on big proddie bikes is a sight and sound to stir the emotion of any biker.

So it was less fun than the R1, was it? John Cantile from *Superbike* shows you can still have fun on a 'Blade – post-R1 or not. (*Superbike*)

The king is dead?

By the end of 1997 it looked as though the Honda FireBlade's five-year reign at the top of the big-bore sportsbike league was coming to an end. The opposition, it seemed, was finally wising up and developing machines that, if the rumours were to be believed, could have the beating of the 'Blade.

By the summer of 1997, sales of Kawasaki's ZX-9R Ninja in its B series form were good, but steady. It was generally accepted that as a usable, very fast sports tourer the bike excelled, but as a cutting-edge super-sports machine it wasn't up to the CBR's standards. But Kawasaki were going to take the development of the new series of the Ninja – the C model – that bit further. Although this machine was to be a total rework, Kawasaki would cleverly retain the name and attractive lines of the original, so as to hopefully take owners of the older machine on to the new bike.

When the ZX-9RC1 finally broke cover at the end of 1997 it looked good. It had an almost shark-like grace to it, as well as a much sportier, trimmed-down feel.

On paper its spec was going to be pretty close to the 'Blade. Lessons had been learned, so that weight was lost in key areas – especially in the chassis department. Compared to the older B4 Ninja, the C1 had

lost 35kg (77.1lb), taking it down to 183kg (403lb) – just three more than the 1998 FireBlade.

As well as the diet, Kawasaki had also done a monster job with the motor. The old model had a stonking kick and an exciting, if harsh, edge to its power delivery – typical of many Kawasakis. The C1 model used a more oversquare bore/stroke ratio, which allowed for less piston speed and therefore more revs. This also helped in finding more room for bigger valves, which allowed more air to get into the motor. All in all, the big K had managed to get a healthy improvement in both power and torque to give the bike around 130bhp at the back wheel.

This added up to a more powerful machine pushing less weight around – just the sort of competition that Honda should have had for the FireBlade years ago.

But the new Kawasaki was just the tip of the iceberg. Quietly, Yamaha had also been looking at the sales of the FireBlade and wanted both a piece of the action and the return of the coveted crown of best big-bore sportsbike.

It had been more than five years since the FZR1000 EXUP held the crown, and as the FZR EXUP-derived Thunderace had been disappointing in the showroom compared to

On paper the new 1998 Kawasaki ZX-9R had the beating of the 'Blade. (Gold and Goose)

Yamaha had learned the lesson well from Honda. The YZF-R1 was an uncompromising machine while the FireBlade had gone soft. (Yamaha UK)

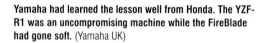

the 'Blade, it was time for Yamaha to strike back.

Initially, when Yamaha's World Superbike race duo of Colin Edwards and Scott Russell were seen testing the bike in the summer of 1997, there was some confusion as to just what capacity this new Yamaha would be. Only in the run-up to that autumn's show season did rumours trickle back to the press that this machine wasn't the long-overdue replacement for the ageing YZF 750 superbike, but was instead a machine that would do what the FZR1000 Genesis and EXUP models had done years before – take the big sportsbike crown for Yamaha.

The specs for the machine were impressive. Yamaha were talking of 155bhp pushing a meagre 177kg (389.9lb) of weight, taking this new sportsbike's performance figures up a notch, and away from the FireBlade. As if this wasn't enough, the performances of other machines in different classes were steadily improving.

Of all the 750 machines in the super-sports class, only the GSX-R750 really came close to the higher capacity machines – despite giving away 150cc. Suzuki's 750 was updated again for the 1998 season, with the addition of a fuel-injection system which replaced the previous GSX-R trait of peaky power delivery with a smooth, linear power curve that still had that 115–120bhp top-end rush. In the 600 super-sports categories machine performance was also coming on in leaps and bounds, with machines like the Kawasaki ZX-6R Ninja being trapped through *Bike* magazine's timing lights at an astounding 168mph (270kph) – faster than any FireBlade the magazine had ever tested. All this doubtless prompted many bike buyers to ask: 'Is a 600cc machine more than enough?'

For Baba-san, it was not so surprising that other manufacturers were at last starting to catch up with the success of the CBR900. 'Quite often I talked with the engineers from other manufacturers,' he says. 'Most of them told me they also wanted to make a bike like our FireBlade, but that it was impossible, as their marketing people said it wouldn't sell. After seeing our success, they could finally start developing what they wanted to produce. I heard that rival manufacturers bought many of our CBR900RR FireBlades to study. So I am proud of it. But it wasn't a surprise to finally see someone manage to catch us up.'

But neither Honda nor Baba-san were going to take this lying down.

The 1998 FireBlade

For the 1998 season they had a newly developed FireBlade of their own, another of those measured two-year leaps that saw Honda steadily improve their machines and keep ahead of the pack.

On paper, the reworked 'Blade did look very good indeed. The major improvements were:

Chassis: Overall weight reduced from 184kg (405.3lb) to 179kg (394.3lb).

Frame: Redesigned for better handling. Tests showed that it was stronger while being 4kg (8.8lb) lighter. Slightly modified box section swingarm for increased strength.

Geometry: Fork yoke offset reduced by 5mm to increase trail and stability. Chunkier, alloy bottom yokes now dual clamped for less weight, but increased strength and rigidity. Steering head moved forward by 5mm, which despite the increased offset gave the same wheelbase as the old model.

Suspension: Modified front fork internals and rear shock and linkage, all to improve damping characteristics.

Brakes: Larger front brake discs – up from 296mm to 310mm – and new four-piston calipers for increased stopping power.

Engine: 80 per cent of the motor was changed from its predecessor. Power was now increased to 128bhp (claimed). Combustion chamber, inlet and exhaust ports reshaped for better gas flow. New metal composite cylinder sleeves for reduced friction and weight. Larger volume radiator for more efficient cooling. Stainless steel exhaust system with bigger silencer to increase power.

Ignition: Remapped digital ignition for better throttle response.

Gearbox: Top gear ratio increased by 2.5 per cent for higher top speed.

Clutch: More compact than previous version, with eight plates to reduce weight and, again, to improve throttle response as the clutch bit.

Electrics: Redesigned headlight, but still retaining the famous FireBlade 'stare'. Thinner, lighter instrument panel. New ignition barrel and switch for improved security.

Styling: Redesigned upper fairing and screen for better aerodynamics and wind protection for the rider. Smoother-styled seat unit. Aluminium top fairing bracket (lighter than previous steel version). Under-seat U-lock holder.

Brits Dave Hancock and Phillip McCallen were again involved with the redesign from its early stages. Hancock first rode the 1998 model 18 months before its launch, once again at the Tochigi proving ground in Japan where the first model was rigorously tested. He spent thousands of miles in the saddle, evaluating every aspect of the bike from how the motor felt, to the brakes' performance, to how effective the dash layout was and how the riding position felt. Other things, such as how easy the bike was to service and even how the toolkit should be designed, were also taken into consideration.

Hancock says: 'We used many of Phillip's comments on the previous bike to improve this model's performance. We found all his experience of riding a FireBlade so hard around the TT course invaluable in bringing the standards of the 'Blade further forward. Improvements in handling and braking were mainly due to Phil's comments.'

'I'd already put some of my ideas into my own FireBlade,' says Phillip (see Chapter 5), 'so I was pleased to see some of the things I did to mine – such as the increased trail/longer frame idea – go into this new 'Blade. It meant that we could steady the steering up, but also keep the same, short wheelbase.'

'Who are you calling old and soft?' Honda's latest FireBlade still retained the aggressive lines of the original, just, but was even easier to ride than ever. (Honda UK)

Rumour has it that some machines from 1998 had a special message for their owners on the inside of the cockpit – it's now become a little bit of FireBlade folklore.

Hancock: 'I think if you check the inside of the top fairing cowling on the left-hand side of the 1998 model, owners will see a message signed by Baba-san himself. It says that the machine was built to help riders appreciate the feeling of power and light weight. He got into trouble for doing that, I think. But Baba being Baba he did it anyway…'

But despite all the improvements and advances, had Honda done enough to keep the opposition at bay? Only an exhaustive back-to-back test of all the models would tell.

All three machines were launched in quick succession in early 1998. Initial launch reports for the Kawasaki saw the world's journalists agreeing that the updated ZX-9R was simply stunning and a quantum leap forward over its predecessor. When the FireBlade took its turn, many again felt that the ingredients had been tweaked enough to make it a better all-round bike. But some complained that it was starting to feel its age compared to its rivals, even before there had been any group tests.

With Honda continually making the FireBlade easier to ride, many felt that the exciting cocktail of unintended wheelies and tank-slapping heroics that made the original a feared, cult machine had been sacrificed, to make it a much easier to ride bike for the masses, and thus no longer the hooligan it once was.

Many thought this was a shame, including the then leading monthly magazine in the UK, *Performance Bikes*, which said 'Has the 'Blade gone soft?' on its front cover. Simon Hargreaves, editor of *PB*, said: 'If these bikes were at school then the 1998 FireBlade is Peter Perfect but the new Yamaha R1 and Kawasaki ZX-9R Ninja are the bad lads. Where the 'Blade was once a vicious thing which would hurt you bad if you messed with it, time and a succession of tweaks and refinements have matured the Honda into – believe it or not – an all rounder. It's been tamed, rounded off and softened by degrees and, although it's more effective than ever before, it's not as wild as it once was. Honda has taken its most mental creation and somehow made it both better and forgettable at the same time.'

Other magazines agreed. Martin Child from *Bike*: 'The FireBlade is even more of a top bike now, but the steering has been calmed down quite a bit. The CBR is no longer the sharp, quick steering bike it once was.'

Martin Port from *Australian Motorcycle News*: 'The first bike was one that wasn't hard to scare yourself shitless with, yet this new bike is less narrowly-focused and more confidence inspiring. Obviously Honda are trying to broaden its rideability capabilities.' Later in the year, *Aussie MCN*'s editor – the respected veteran journalist Ken Wootton – said: 'All the changes to this new model seem to make the bike more predictable, neutral and rideable. In fact Honda had neutralised the CBR to a point that it lost a little of the raw appeal which originally made the bike such an international success.'

Kiwi Rider's Jonathan Bentman: 'The 'Blade has become remarkably civilised for 1998. I guess it's a measure of how advanced the original machine was that it's taken some six years for the competition to at last develop serious opposition – despite Honda's efforts – in the meantime – to effectively mellow the 'Blade. But competition the FireBlade now most certainly has, in the forms of the Kawasaki ZX-9R, the Yamaha R1 and the (remarkably overlooked) fuel-injected Suzuki GSX-R750W.'

Motor Cyclist in the USA managed to get a new Kawasaki ZX-9R Ninja and a CBR900RR together for the first time as early as their March 1998 issue. 'The old gal was a rampaging party beast at her launch in mid 1992,' it reported, 'and since then she's evolved into the smoothest, sweetest comfortablest, all-round *nicest* device capable of turning your eyes skyward at a twist of the throttle. Let us praise Honda and Mr Baba for refining it year after year because progress is a good thing. Now then, will someone wheel the old dear out of the way so we can get on with praising our newest idol? It's taken other manufacturers six years but the wait is over. Something Kawasaki green is knocking on the door.'

Motor Cyclist also felt that the Honda had lost

its edge, lost its sharp appeal. 'While the Honda is at home organising its sock drawer,' they said, 'the Kawasaki is out drinking beers with the boys in the garage. That's how the two stack up against each other on the road, too. Where the CBR offers linear, smooth and easily modulatable power delivery, the ZX draws a line in the sand with its toe and dares you to cross it. It sort of gargles and spits, off idle, like a constipated camel or top fuel dragster before exploding into the first level of its powerband at 4,500rpm or so.'

Constipated camels aside, the big Kwak was exciting, harsh, almost scary – like the old FireBlade.

Back Down Under, *Australian Motorcycle News* put a ZX-9R head-to-head with a FireBlade and it showed just what a close call it could be. 'If the rear suspension came fully dialled in, I'd take the Kawasaki,' explained Martin Port, 'but out of the crate I'll take the keys to the Honda.' Ken Wootton went the

'It was the best FireBlade yet', said McCallen of the 1998 CBR. (Gold and Goose)

other way. 'Quite simply the extra 20 horses and the fabulous Kawasaki induction roar push the odds in the Ninja's favour.'

Unfortunately for the Honda, not only did it have to take on the raucous Kawasaki, it also eventually had to come up against the mighty Yamaha YZF-R1.

Even in isolation the launch reports for the all-new R1 were stunning. In their search for superlatives journalists harked back to the days of 1992, when the first FireBlade was launched, or back even further, to the launch of the Kawasaki GPz900R. It really was that good.

Yamaha launched the R1 at Cartagena in Spain. It's a track not normally considered perfect for a litre-sized sportsbike, as it contains 14 twists and turns and a small start/finish straight within its 2.1-mile (3.4km) length. Yamaha, though, wanted to use a track that would show just how good the bike was through the corners, rather than just somewhere that the 998cc powerplant and excellent one-piece, four-piston calipers could shine.

Bike magazine's Olly Duke was beside himself after riding the bike. 'After a day's riding

at Cartagena I have to say the R1's everything it's cracked up to be and much, much more. Every journalist rode away from the track launch in awe of the Yamaha. It turns in quick and tracks through the corners with complete precision and makes 600s and 750s obsolete.'

The first full group tests between the major players saw the R1 come out on top. *Bike* magazine took the FireBlade, Yamaha R1, Kawasaki ZX-9R Ninja and Triumph's T595i down to the South of France for a long-distance blast, taking in Folembray circuit on the way. Road test editor Olly Duke said in his report: 'For heaven's sake, what's happened to the FireBlade we all knew and loved and were secretly afraid of, the twitchy on-the-edge sportster that spawned a thousand bar-room stories? Over the years it's become softer and softer and this test makes the 'Blade seem softer still.'

And of the R1: 'It's the detail touches that tell you the R1 is something special. When you own this, you know you have the best engine, the best chassis, the best brakes, the best suspension, the best looker. The R1 is not just better than the other machines in this test, it's light years ahead of them.' *Bike*'s resident two-wheeled stuntman Martin Child agreed: 'Anybody expecting me to buck the trend by slating Yamaha's YZF-R1 will be sadly disappointed. Very disappointed. Quite simply it's the pinnacle of two-wheel entertainment. More acceleration, quicker response and far superior handling to any other bike I've ever ridden. At any revs in any gear the R1 is pulling in the horizon faster than the poor little horizon has ever been pulled. The bike even looks ballistic standing still.'

Superbike magazine placed the FireBlade fifth in its annual sportsbike of the year competition. Editor Grant Leonard said: 'This sportsbike of the year stuff is all very well, but the bottom line is that the FireBlade will outsell the lot of them despite this test. Why? Because it's got six years behind it of reputation, accolades, achievements and reliability. It's the next biggest icon after Harley-Davidson. And that counts for lots. However, for spoilt-brat journalists it counts for nothing and if we can go faster on a ZX9R or an R1 we'll bin the

'Blade. The FireBlade is history.'

Australian Motorcycle News put on a mammoth test complete with all the major big-bore sportsbike opposition of 1998 – the Honda CBR900RR FireBlade, Kawasaki ZX-9R Ninja, Yamaha YZF-R1, Suzuki TL1000R, Ducati 996 Biposto, and Triumph 955i. The test included three days of solid road-riding and a day at the challenging Phillip Island circuit. In earlier days this was the sort of test in which the FireBlade would have romped home the winner. But now all seven riders voted for the Yamaha R1 (although many expressed a preference for the Ducati, if someone else was paying!).

Back home in Japan the reputation of the FireBlade was also under threat from the R1. Satoshi Kogure from *Young Machine* magazine: 'The awesome R1 was a true nightmare for avid FireBlade fans and also for Honda. I don't need to mention here how good the Yamaha R1 was, you've heard all about it and you know, but this export-only bike was also a success in Japan as well as around the world. It sold much better than CBR900RR in the debut year, and *Young Machine* readers chose the Yamaha YZF-R1 as the "Machine of The Year 1998", a prize which the Honda CBR900RR FireBlade had never won in six or seven years. And look at the Isle of Man results from 1999! It is expected that every year a FireBlade will win the production race and 'Blade fans in Japan were expecting the CBR900RR Evolution to beat the R1s very badly, but the result was very disappointing. I remember thinking at the time that it couldn't be worse. In my opinion people in the world witnessed the death of the FireBlade there on a little island in the Irish Sea. The top selling and top performing spot is what both the FireBlade and Honda lived for and in those categories people found the machine's true value. To be second best means nothing. It is sad, but true. This is the fate of these kinds of bikes.'

Despite the criticism from the press about the 'softened' 1998 FireBlade, the way the design of the bike had moved over the years was down to individuals much more important than any journalist.

It was the buying public that had wanted more comfort and less of an 'edge' to the 'Blade. Throughout the FireBlade's reign as

Australian Motorcycle News again tested old and new side by side. 'More predictable, neutral and rideable', said editor Wootton. (*AMCN*)

top-selling big-bore sportsbike, Dave Hancock had spoken to thousands of owners, and he was in no doubt as to what they wanted.

'Some people would complain that the bike made their arms ache,' he recalls, 'so we moved the bars a bit higher and over the years really refined the ergonomics to suit more people. That's what we've done, made the bike easier to ride and that's a good thing as more people can get to grips with the FireBlade. During the life of the 'Blade that's all we've ever been doing – listening to our customers. The sales bear it out. We've sold more every year, even as we've "softened" the bike's feel. I admit that this can have a detrimental effect, though, as we found a little with the VFR programme. As you refine the bike and make it better sometimes you can end up losing some of the original bike's character. The VFR is a good example. I really loved the later 750 versions of the VFR but found that although the latest fuel-injected VFR800 is a better bike I still think more fondly of the older model. I think

that was what happened with the later versions of the 'Blade.

'The good thing about the R1 coming out was that our engineers could now get a look at it and begin developing something better. Previously all we'd been able to do was listen to rumours or second guess the opposition as to what they were developing. Now we could see what we had to beat. Honda has always amazed me at just how they look at and scrutinise someone's product and then go and make something even better. That's why I think that even though the Yamaha YZF-R1 is a brilliant bike and has finally caught up with the FireBlade, this just means that we can now take that machine and make something even better than that. To be honest, of all the 1998 bikes I personally rated the Kawasaki above the R1. In tests I found it to be a much better road bike than the R1, much more playing the FireBlade's game.'

McCallen felt that the press reaction to the latest version was a little too critical.

Stemming the tide
Honda Britain's Evolution FireBlade

There was a FireBlade that could take on Yamaha's impressive YZF-R1 – and win. It came at a price. A price of between £22,000 and £25,000, depending on whether you wanted the 'cheap' or 'pricey' version.

It was the Honda TT100 Evolution FireBlade, an official 'special' built at the end of 1998 to celebrate Honda's 100th victory in the Isle of Man TT races, won by Jim Moodie on a FireBlade in the Production Race.

The machine debuted at that year's International Motorcycle Show at Birmingham's NEC, and was well received by crowds at the show, even if they had a major coronary at the price tag. The brains behind it were ex-racer turned Honda-bod Mick Grant and respected tuner Russell Savory. Both had been working together in the RS Performance/Sanyo Honda team, which the previous year had taken Paul 'Marra' Brown to the 600 title and the British Powerbike Series title the year after, with Steve Plater on a Savory-tuned FireBlade.

The bike was a brutish masterpiece. It still looked very much like a 'Blade, but now had a more purposeful appearance, with its exposed single-sided swingarm and two huge fresh air scoops

The Evolution FireBlade was an awesome bit of kit, but very expensive. (Roland Brown)

near the screen.

No expense was spared, either, when it came to the spec of this 'new' machine. Better breathing for the engine was the key to the CBR's extra power. The two huge ducts above the headlights pushed large amounts of air into the large-volume airbox. Carbs in the Evo were 41mm Keihin flat-slides and the exhaust was a four-into-one titanium model with a Micron carbon oval silencer. All the major internals such as pistons, con-rods, and crankshaft were balanced. The cylinder head was ported and gas-flowed. RS Performance high-lift cams operated standard valves closed by RS springs. The standard gearbox was junked in favour of a close-ratio one, similar to that used by Plater in his 1998 Powerbike season. A new ignition box helped the machine peak at a 12,200rpm limit, as shown on a flashy LCD Stack dash. RS Performance quoted power as 165bhp at the crank with 150bhp at the rear wheel. That compares to a standard machine on the same dyno pumping out 118bhp. Impressive.

Suspension parts were just as flash. Ohlins 43mm

inverted racing forks at the front and an Ohlins unit at the rear working on a single-sided swingarm. Brakes were Brembo's racing finest (four calipers and 320mm discs at the front). Wheels were lightweight Dymags and tyres (the front was a 17-incher) were Dunlop D207s. The bodywork was sculpted by leading bike designer John Keogh, mimicking the original, but smoothing out the whole shape a little. Owners would get front and rear paddock stands, a riding jacket, a bike cover plus a data sheet including all recommended suspension settings for road and track. Alternative parts, such as single and twin seats (touring on *this*?) and high and low-slung exhaust systems in road or race form, completed your return for the £22,325 outlay. And if you wanted to spend more, a £25,000 'Stealth' version came with fuel-injection, carbon-fibre bodywork, magnesium single sided swingarm and carbon Dymag wheels.

Celebrating Moodie's success on the Island wasn't the Evo FireBlade's sole *raison d'être*. It also had another reason to be produced.

Despite Plater's title and Moodie's TT victory, Honda UK must have felt that the 1998 version of the FireBlade would have a hard time of it up against the R1 in the Isle of Man TT races and in production racing during 1999, so a trick 'official' FireBlade could race in the standard model's stead – as long as the bike was homologated for racing by the UK's racing chiefs in the Motorcycle Circuit Racing Control Board. (That's why the EvoBlade's tank was blown to handle 23.5 litres of fuel, instead of 18, so now it could easily do two flying laps of the 37.73 mile TT circuit…).

Almost immediately the opposition started to complain, arguing (quite rightly) that it went against the spirit of production racing. 'If the Evolution FireBlade is let in,' said Yamaha UK's Jeff Turner, 'it will ruin production racing overnight.' Yamaha even threatened to quit production racing in 1999 if the Evo was made eligible to race – despite winning the Production Championship that year with an R1.

Eventually it wasn't allowed to race anyway, because the 150 road-going bikes needed for homologation purposes had not been built in time for the March '99 deadline.

Savory was disappointed at the decision.

'We could have appealed against the decision by the MCRCB,' he said, 'but instead we decided to concentrate on the challenge for the 600 title – which every year is vitally important for Honda.'

Turner said: 'We're pleased at the decision, but really the whole issue of production racing

The men behind the bike: Russell Savory (left) and Mick Grant. (Roland Brown)

regulations should be looked at and hopefully they will be tightened up so manufacturers and specials builders know where they stand and whether their machines qualify.'

As if all this wasn't bad enough, Harley-Davidson was also investigating whether they had sole copyright over the use of the words Evolution and Evo, used on the new V-twin motors which were powering some of their latest machines.

The bike was nevertheless a stunner, amazing to behold and to ride, but without a reason to be built not a great many were sold. Who knows, maybe one day they'll become collectors' items.

MCN's Chris Moss gets down to it on the '98 íBlade. Even if it didn't have the edge on the R1 technologically, it still did in the showrooms early that year... *(MCN)*

'Quite simply it's the best FireBlade ever,' he says. 'I think people's views were a little coloured with the introduction of the R1. Sure, the R1 is an excellent bike and better performance wise in many respects to the 'Blade, but it did take the competition six years and still the CBR was competitive and selling more.'

But despite the sudden eclipse of the CBR900RR FireBlade the bike continued to sell more and more than ever. It remained the biggest selling big-bore sports machine in the UK in 1998 – although the R1 wasn't released until a little after the '98 model 'Blade. There were rumours of Honda UK shifting ready registered machines to surprised dealers but these were unsubstantiated.

Whatever. In the UK, 2,866 CBR900RRs were sold in 1997, and the new model proved to be even more popular, with 3,832 sold during the course of 1998.

The start of 1999 saw sales still good and steady – a total of 2,380 up until the end of August – making a total of 17,132 FireBlades sold in the UK since launch in 1992. But now there was a different name on top of the sales charts.

It was, perhaps, to be expected that with the press claiming a new king of sportsbike performance, sales would eventually start to turn in the Yamaha's favour. And so it was that, for the first time in seven years, a name other than that of the Honda CBR900RR FireBlade topped the charts.

To have been finally caught up by Yamaha wasn't anything to be ashamed about. On the contrary, the FireBlade design team and Baba-san himself were almost pleased to suddenly be on the back foot.

He says: 'Well, it was almost flattering! The

engineers of our rivals obviously recognised our work as epoch-making. Now we felt like we were the ones who opened up the market first. Our philosophy has always been that the bike has to be lighter and more controllable, but still affordable. If I had a choice between 10bhp or reducing weight by 10kg I would reduce the weight, because that way you keep the same basic concept of the RR, which is total human control. I was most pleased when others began to follow the concept of our CBR900RR. Our concept of a lightweight, easily controllable machine was well understood by most manufacturers and that made me very happy. I was very surprised at the high specification of the Yamaha R1. When it first came out I remember thinking what a nice bike it looked. I was eager to ride it as soon as possible after its launch. As engineers, we could look at both the

Kawasaki and the Yamaha machines and work very hard to try to get our share back and take the new FireBlade on to even greater heights.

'When people asked me about the direction that the new FireBlade would go in I had to be very careful when answering the questions: "What will the capacity be?" "Will it be a completely different bike?" "How about the chassis? Will there be big improvements there?" All I would say was that we do have something special, but I cannot say it here! Trust us. Please wait and we will make all your dreams come true!'

The bike that would be spawned from both the 'old' CBR900RR and the opposition would be ready for launch at the turn of the millennium. It would be a machine worthy of the name FireBlade.

The slimmed down rear-end will still carry a U-lock for security and your partner on tour. (Honda)

Fifth generation the millennium 'Blade

He who has the sharpest blade, fights fewest battles…

With its rivals finally taking the limelight, performance edge, and finally sales away from the FireBlade, something had to be done.

Rumours of fuel-injection, ram-air, and a big-bore 1,000cc version of the CBR were all rife, but when the new machine finally broke cover at the end of 1999, although it looked initially very different to the previous models, beneath the skin it was the age-old Honda dictum of 'evolution not revolution.'

Again Baba was at the head of the team which was undertaking the FireBlade's biggest revamp yet. Right from the outset he knew in which direction he wanted to take the 'Blade, and it wasn't to attack the R1 head on with a bike that had a similar uncompromising feel. It still had to have a CBR's feel, its usability and heritage.

'It always surprises me,' says Baba-san, 'that expensive parts, or maybe those made with unrealistic performance in mind today, will appear on the motorcycles of tomorrow. Just

like the advancement of the computer industry, bit by bit, bike design must move on. Even with this in mind, we knew the latest CBR had to prioritise "humanity", or how a person really feels on the bike, not just the latest engineering, materials, or maximum performance. For example, how we make the bike react to your right arm movement – whether it's the throttle, the brakes, or the steering – is much more important than putting the most expensive high-performance parts on the machine. What good are the latest parts if you cannot use them or work in harmony with them? Brakes that perform too well can be too much for the rider, so too can an engine that has too much power. If the functions work too directly, it can be too much for a human being.

'So, what we decided to do was to study more about the human being, as well as the engineering. I'm sure that not only human engineering, but also human mentality, will be more important for all industrial products of the future. We have to examine how we can put this humanity and engineering together. We

also have to think about the environment a lot more when considering motorcycle manufacture. So we had to develop a system that cleans the exhaust gas. That's what we have to work at seriously now as well. We have to introduce these environment-friendly parts without disturbing the performance or upsetting the balance of the machine. This is what we looked at when shaping the overall feel of the latest CBR900.'

Once more Baba's skills as both a project leader and a test rider were needed to bring the CBR up to date with the competition. He says: 'We still found many things which we couldn't calculate on a computer – no matter how far we've advanced. Sometimes we found that, say, the computer was telling us that one plus one was two. Sometimes it's not! Think

about it. On a bike you may find that some parts work to 70 per cent of their efficiency, some parts work to 90 per cent, some parts work to 20 per cent, and the resulting whole is a bike that reacts at 80 per cent. We have to find out what the best setting is for all these variables. This is something you can't calculate on the computer. And you can't write it down on a piece of paper to work it out. To know it, to really understand it and be able to change it, you have to ride the development machine over and over again.'

And so the process started again. Like ancient Japanese swordsmiths, Baba and his team once more had to hone the FireBlade. The edge could not be too sharp, as the inexperienced could not then wield the blade. Always the rider was foremost in his mind.

Development concept

When the press finally saw the new 'Blade, it confirmed the Honda ethos of increased performance through two-year evolutionary changes. Striving for a total balance of performance, weight has been trimmed, friction has been reduced, power increased and handling sharpened, all while carefully maintaining the FireBlade's reputation for a well-rounded blend of ease of riding and exhilaration which can be enjoyed by a wide cross-section of riders.

The 'new' FireBlade has again been guided by the central theme of 'total control', the same design ethos which had made it Honda's high-performance flagship and gave it its international standing as one of the best sellers in its big-bike displacement class.

Motivated by the simply stated, but uncompromising new development theme of 'lightest and rightest', Baba-san and Honda R&D worked to develop an astounding machine which would boast 'jet fighter-like manoeuvring potential' and astoundingly light weight which would rival nearly all the machines in the 600cc class.

According to the press pack hype, the new FireBlade would 'seem like an integral extension of the rider's very being, all the while retaining and improving upon the old CBR's strengths of renowned user-friendliness and ease of use.'

Styling concept

The first thing that strikes you is the emperor's new clothes. The new CBR900RR FireBlade features all-new bodywork that tries to accentuate a look of lighter weight while closely following the new lines of its all-new aluminium twin-spar frame. Dominating the front end of the machine is the wide new single headlight assembly, which features three bulbs backed by a multi-reflector lens. Low-beam is handled by the bright, middle bulb while high beam sees all three powerful halogen bulbs in use.

With a more compact nose than previous models and curvaceous lines that show influences from the latest CBR600F, the new FireBlade's fairing presents a small forward silhouette that helps the machine cut through the air quickly and efficiently. Rather than completely hiding the frame, the front fairing, fuel tank, and seat cowl take on separate identities that conform with and highlight the new curves of the twin-spar frame.

This sleek, semi-modular design also draws visual attention to the FireBlade's lighter weight by revealing areas of space that provide a balancing and lightening effect to make the entire machine look lighter than it really is – a trick used by the original model back in 1992.

The design team wanted to keep the CBR's comfortable riding position, so, despite the slimmer look, the overall compactness of the new design allied with the frontal aspect actually gives the rider more protection from the elements and conditions.

At the back end the FireBlade's distinctive over/under dual-bulb taillight is retained as an easily distinguished indicator of the CBR's unique lineage, while indicators also feature a multi-reflector design hopefully for easier recognition by myopic car drivers over longer distances.

Despite its slimmed-down rear end the FireBlade is still as practical as ever, featuring as it does a locking rear pillion seat designed to provide a secure and convenient carrying space for assorted riding necessities, including virtually all sizes of 'U'-type security lock or cable lock. Also gone are the five-spoke wheels of old, replaced instead with new black-painted triple-spoke wheels.

But despite all the changes the 'Blade still retains its squat, purposeful look.

The FireBlade's new heart

For several years the engine powering the CBR900RR had received gradual evolutionary changes that had increased its power in a series of small but effective stages.

But the boffins at Honda R&D felt that they'd gone as far as they could with the 'old' motor. What they wanted to do now was give the 918.5cc powerplant a complete redesign, with the goal in mind of producing Yamaha YZF-R1-threatening power.

Several fundamental improvements lurk in its newly designed crankcases, which have been shortened in order to bring the crankshaft and

The new millennium FireBlade in action. Light and powerful,
it is its father's son. Oh, and it is probably a test rider
wearing Mick Doohan's kit – not the man himself! (Honda)

The new three-headlight front-end still shares that 'Blade-esque look. (Honda)

swingarm pivot a full 20mm (0.8in) closer to the front of the bike. This modification achieves three important goals. First, a shorter engine can be moved farther forward in the chassis to concentrate more weight toward the front wheel for better all-round handling and quicker turning. Second, the swingarm can then be lengthened for more progressive rear suspension operation (as Yamaha did first with its 500cc grands prix bikes and later with the road-going YZF-R1) while maintaining exactly the same wheelbase. And third, positioning the swingarm pivot closer to the countershaft helps reduce strain on the drivechain to the wheel as the swingarm moves through its full

suspension movement. This has the knock-on effect of giving the new 'Blade a smoother power transfer to the rear wheel in most riding regimes.

Also contributing to this handling advantage is a new swingarm pivot, cast into the rear of the crankcase as the integral part of a direct mounting system which is similar to (but a bit different from) Honda's current crop of 'pivotless' frame designs, such as the Varadero, CBR600F, and VTR1000 FireStorm.

So, the motor's more compact and positioned further forward to help handling, but what's different inside?

An important factor in gaining improvement

Thankfully, big, bad, butch black and gunmetal made a comeback in Honda's palette. (Honda)

in the CBR's acceleration and overall performance was a change in its engine's cylinder configuration. For more power and higher-revving performance, the engine received a larger bore and shorter stroke, while every effort was made to minimise its overall width and weight. One benefit resulting from the larger bore size is larger valve sizes, and with them greater amounts of air flowing through the combustion chambers for more power.

However, that's not the only change made to the valves. High compression is another critical factor in the power and performance equation and, generally, the most effective means of increasing compression is to narrow the 'squish' area between the piston and the roof of the combustion chamber. Making the chamber as compact as possible necessitated shallower valve angles to reduce the height of the combustion chamber roof. Therefore, the included angle of the larger intake valves was reduced from 16° on the old model to 12° on the new motor, while the angle for the exhaust valves was reduced from 16° to 13°, not only achieving a higher compression ratio but also higher power output, while also improving the all-important torque of the motor.

Moving these valves are a pair of new hollow camshafts that are 20 per cent lighter than the items they replace. Their lighter weight and greatly reduced mass also make a significant contribution to the engine's sharper response (less weight and mass means it's easier to spin a motor to higher rpm, and more quickly). And although the sum total of these modifications also resulted in a taller head design, the cylinders' 4mm reduction in stroke more than compensated for the increase, resulting in minimal changes to the engine's overall height – remember, a tall motor means too much mass and weight at the extremities, which is not good for 'total control' or 'mass centralisation'.

Another factor that has a strong impact on engine performance is the weight of the pistons themselves. For the new FireBlade, high-precision forged aluminium pistons replace the cast aluminium units used on previous models. Computer-assisted engineering (CAE) was also used in their design process and manufacture to remove or retain material from the underside of the pistons depending on where structural strength was required. So, even though the new pistons are larger in diameter than the ones they replace, their weight is almost exactly the same. As in the current CBR, these pistons pump through lightweight metal composite cylinder sleeves, formed of sintered aluminium powder impregnated with tough ceramic and graphite for reduced friction and excellent heat dissipation, to ensure cooler operation with longevity.

Fuel-injection

Not all of the hoo-ha surrounding the new CBR was pure hokum. The safe money was always on some form of fuel-injection, and after introducing the system on the CBR1100XX Blackbird and VFR Honda finally felt that it was ready for its flagship mass-produced sports model.

The PGM-FI programmed fuel injection unit is the latest high-performance, computer-controlled system. Its advanced electronic design integrates both the fuel injection system's electronic control unit (ECU) and the CBR's digital electronic ignition into a single compact 'black box' for precise fuel metering and combustion control. Specially tuned to

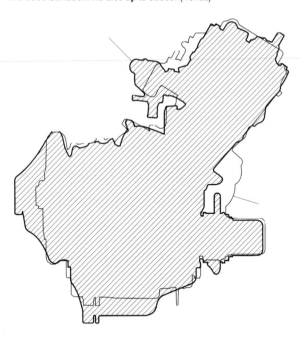

Lighter and more compact than the previous model's motor, the 2000 CBR900RR is also up to 929cc. (Honda)

give the FireBlade the most responsive performance over a wide range of operating conditions, it is also responsible for remarkably low fuel consumption figures and – in a special system for the German market – some of the lowest exhaust emissions figures ever attained in a big-bore sportsbike. As introduced on last year's fuel-injected CBR1100XX Super Blackbird, the FireBlade's fuel injection system also features an automatic bypass starter system that ensures smooth performance and quick starts in varying weather conditions.

Honda intake and exhaust powervalve system

To maximise the FireBlade's power over its entire engine speed range, a new electrically operated valve system was developed to control the volumes of both its intake and exhaust flow.

Dubbed the Honda Variable Intake/Exhaust Control System, or H-VIX, this system features a large flap valve in the aircleaner that opens and closes at pre-set engine speeds to increase or decrease the volume of air reaching the fuel injection system, depending on the engine's range of operation, while maintaining optimal intake velocity over the entire rpm range. The large-volume aircleaner's intake duct has also been designed to access a steady supply of cool, dense air from deep inside the front fairing and away from the heat of the engine and radiator. The second half of this innovative system features a special valve box built into the exhaust system's collector that optimises the engine's power characteristics at both low and high revs. This newly developed Honda titanium exhaust valve (H-TEV) provides the scavenging and related power benefits of a 360° exhaust collector design at low to mid-range engine speeds, then switches at a pre-set engine speed to an effective 180° collector design to maintain optimum power characteristics at high rpms. This system sounds very similar to Yamaha's EXUP powervalve system, which has been on that manufacturer's machines for the last decade. The combined effect of these two systems ensures optimum intake and exhaust flow for the highest performance at both low and high rpms, with no compromises.

The year 2000 CBR also features a titanium exhaust downpipe, which is normally only seen on race exhaust systems and Kawasaki's ZX-9R. The titanium extends down to the H-TEV power valve system and is also used in the baffle of the end can, which features an aluminium canister. Linking the two sections is a large-diameter length of stainless steel tubing that feeds all the way into the silencer. Not only is the system the lightest and strongest ever for a 'Blade, it is also responsible for a significant share of the FireBlade's new boost in power output.

That power output now goes through a gearbox with an overall 5 per cent reduction in its transmission gear ratios that optimises the engine's performance at cruising speeds while delivering an exciting blast of acceleration from virtually anywhere in the FireBlade's wide powerband.

The important figures are these: 929cc, a shade over 150bhp at the crank, meaning around 135bhp at the rear wheel – well within striking distance of the R1, especially as the new CBR is also 13kg (28.6lb) lighter than the old model and 7kg (15.4lb) lighter than the YZF-R1.

Lean, mean, green machine

As Baba-san has said, the new Honda CBR900RR FireBlade has to be eco-friendly as well as being able to outperform the opposition. So, a number of technological advantages – some old, some new – have been combined to make the FireBlade one of the 'greenest' internal-combustion engined two-wheelers on the planet.

The 'Blade is equipped with Honda's most up-to-date low emissions exhaust system, the Honda evolutional catalysing system – or HECS3 on its German version. Taking advantage of the high-accuracy computerised control of the FireBlade's new PGM-FI fuel injection unit, the system features a high-sensitivity oxygen sensor installed in the exhaust system and a compact cylindrical catalyser element built into the silencer's stainless steel inlet tube to reduce exhaust pollution levels to below those currently required by both Europe's EURO-1 emissions regulations and Germany's stricter Summer Smog 2 (SS-2) regulations.

In detail, the motor's eco-friendly components are:

Air injection: In the interests of minimising exhaust emissions, the FireBlade features a built-in air injection system that helps complete the burning of exiting exhaust gases. Essentially the same system as featured on the CBR600F and CBR1100XX Super Blackbird and machines from other Japanese manufacturers – such as Suzuki's GSX1300R Hayabusa and the Kawasaki ZX-9R – this direct air injection system ensures compliance with Europe's current EURO-1 emissions regulations.

High accuracy exhaust oxygen sensor: Similar to the system currently featured on other Honda models like the CBR1100XX Super Blackbird and the VFR, the FireBlade's fuel injection control unit (ECU) accurately monitors several variables of engine operation in order to ensure precise fuel control. One critical factor is the constantly fluctuating level of oxygen present in the engine's exhaust gases, which is checked by a highly sensitive 'O2 feedback' sensor installed in the exhaust system just before the CBR's silencer.

This highly accurate system maintains the air/fuel ratio within a close range of tolerance centred around the optimal ratio of 14.7:1. At this ratio, the catalyser element performs at its highest efficiency to achieve a minimised balance of hydrocarbons (HC) and carbon monoxide (CO) on the one hand and nitrous oxides (NOX) on the other. Improvements in the accuracy of the fuel injection ECU also help extend this optimal balance of low emissions over a wider range of operating conditions than previously possible.

Compact three-way catalyser: The final component in the system is a compact catalyser element installed in the exhaust system immediately before the FireBlade's end-can. This cylindrical 'three-way' element completes the system's high-efficiency exhaust cleansing operation by chemically neutralising and eliminating the emissions of CO, HC, and NOX gases from the exhaust flowing through it.

Chassis developments

Honda R&D's relentless pursuit of lighter weight also extends to the new CBR's frame and chassis, and the result is an unprecedented new design that not only realises lighter weight, but also a more highly tuned balance of rigidity for precise and easy control. The new aluminium twin-spar frame's triple-box-section main spars reach back from a massive steering head casting to join at a large rear casting that also provides a supporting arm for the rear suspension's damper. The spars themselves not only curve back to provide a narrower profile in the seat area, they also taper upward to meet the lines of the CBR's narrower and outwardly smaller new fuel tank with a unique, flush-surface shape. Solidly gripping the engine in a multi-point diamond configuration, this main section of the frame is 30 per cent more rigid than the previous model, while the engine's more compact design permits the steering head and front wheel to be located closer to the machine's centre of mass for better turning ability.

Making a frame that is too rigid is not what Honda wanted to do. Some race bikes from the early 'nineties found that a frame that is too rigid fails to give the rider enough feedback on what is happening at speed and can be unsettling in certain situations.

With this firmly in mind, the new CBR was designed to permit a precisely controlled amount of torsional cornering forces to bend the frame slightly at a specially selected point near its centre of mass for greatly enhanced handling and feedback to the rider. This is all a throwback to what Baba wanted for the bike. The whole bike must be usable and should not overwhelm the rider.

Mass centralisation… again

Another goal in the design of the new 'Blade was the continuation of the mass centralisation theme. This is partially achieved in the new CBR by both the positioning of the engine within the twin spars of the frame, as well as in such details as the positioning of its fuel tank. The CBR's fuel tank carries a full 18 litres (31.7gal), the same as its predecessor, and that's a heavy load to be slinging around when perched high up in the frame. The CBR's new frame is narrower in the seat area, but room was still made to extend the main volume of the fuel tank lower at its rear, and so closer to the machine's centre of mass. This permitted the outer dimensions of the tank to be reduced in size, with fully 10mm (0.39in) trimmed from its height and 40mm (1.57in) taken off its length. The fuel tank also receives a more rounded profile that conforms closely with the new curves in the frame's spars, meaning that more people of different shapes and sizes can feel comfortable with the combination of tank shape, longer seat, and shorter and easier reach to the handlebars.

Also in the interests of less weight, the new FireBlade features a lighter and slimmer, fully electronic, one-piece meter panel that cleanly and simply connects to the wiring harness by way of a single connector, with no bundles of wires and cables to contend with. This all-new, fully enclosed unit fits behind the fairing cowl and displays a large, white-face tachometer and a high-accuracy digital LCD speedometer/odometer/trip meter display. The

The latest synthesis of Baba-san's 'total control' philosophy, including ecologically friendlier motor and semi-pivotless frame. (Honda)

panel also features a low fuel warning light and an ignition key confirmation indicator LED for the 'Blade's new HISS anti-theft system. Like several other recent models, the 'Blade's HISS system uses an electronic interlock to prevent the engine from being started by any other than the motorcycle's two original keys.

Since the HISS disables the motorcycle at the heart of its ignition system, it cannot be bypassed by either hot-wiring the ignition or exchanging the ignition switch module. A bright yellow diamond-shaped HISS sticker on the top of the fuel tank clearly indicates the presence of this system to warn off potential thieves.

Even the electrical system has felt the effects of the FireBlade's emphasis on lighter weight. Since all electrical components place a load on the system, and the FireBlade's new fuel-injection system and fuel pump add to that load, rather than increasing the size of the ACG, with its accompanying weight and size cutting into performance, the draw of other components – in particular the headlight – was reduced to compensate. In low beam mode, the single H7 headlight places less of a load on the electrical system than the dual bulb system it replaces, while its reflector was redesigned to optimise its output. The high beam, on the other hand, which is used less often, features three H7 bulbs producing a brilliant range of illumination with little change in total load from the dual bulb system used on the previous CBR. Even the battery – which was tiny anyway – has been reduced in size, and its innovative new design achieves a 10 per cent increase in output to produce the same rating with a considerable reduction in size and weight.

Semi-pivotless frame design

A fundamental feature of the FireBlade's new frame is its 'semi-pivotless' design, which combines elements of Honda's pioneering 'pivotless' frame design to reduce both the weight and torsional stresses associated with conventional pivot plates, which sit at the end of the frame rails and attach to the swingarm pivot. However, while the FireBlade's massive new swingarm does have its pivot point at the rear of the engine, its lower frame design deviates radically from most other modern bikes.

Like the 'pivotless' design, the main body of the frame does not reach all the way down to the swingarm pivot, so it is effectively isolated from the stresses exerted by the swingarm during hard acceleration and cornering. However, a large casting reaches across underneath the pivot to solidly grip the ends of the swingarm pivot shaft, and lock it solidly into alignment with the engine. This separation of the main frame and the swingarm permits a more easily tuned match to the engine's power and weight characteristics, as well as meaning that it's easier to set the machine up for varying rider sizes and riding styles, whether on road or track.

Suspension

Back in 1992, European test riders begged Baba and his development team for 'fashionable' upside-down or inverted telescopic forks to be used on the first version of the CBR900RR, but he said no on the grounds that they were just too heavy.

Remember what Baba-san said above about time moving on and parts and materials developing at a pace? Well, now he and the design team have seen fit for the first time ever to equip a road-bike – the year 2000 FireBlade – with inverted front forks.

Honda used the same lightweight fork

Gone are the standard forks and 16-inch front wheel. The latest technology means Honda finally use light, inverted forks and a 17-incher. (Honda)

developing techniques that served them well in the past on the CBR900 project and applied them to inverted forks. The design team felt that inverted fork technology had come along well enough in the last couple of years to warrant testing for use on the new CBR. Following extensive testing covering several variations of the inverted fork design, the team selected a new 43mm cartridge-type set that offers lighter weight than ever achieved in this type of fork, as well as smoother, more dependable performance. The forks are gripped by meaty, forged aluminium triple-clamps.

If any one thing really grabs attention on the new CBR900RR FireBlade, it will most certainly be its all-new aluminium swingarm. With its fundamental design based on lessons learned in the development of HRC's all-conquering NSR500, which has been the most successful 500cc GP bike of the last decade, this radical new swingarm features a massive, multi-tapered cast right-side member and pivot mount coupled to a large, triple-box-section extruded left-side member that is supported by a welded-on Yagura brace for rigidity and strength. As mentioned briefly earlier, the engine's reduced crankshaft-to-pivot dimensions freed up room to extend the length

Honda CBR900RR FireBlade Day Silverstone, June 2000

More than 4,000 people turned up for the inaugural Honda FireBlade day on more than 2,000 FireBlades. To celebrate this milestone machine, Honda organised the use of the Silverstone international circuit, as well as planning FireBlade workshops, stands selling FireBlade goods, FireBlade specials complete with their very special owners, round-the-world FireBlades, race FireBlades, road FireBlades, and many more.

Some of Honda's race teams – including the Castrol Honda Supersport 600 team and the Harris Honda Superbike were also present, and 'Blade nuts loved it.

Dave Hailstone from Milton Keynes spent most of his day enjoying himself while his immaculate N-reg Urban Tiger 'Blade was shot in a makeshift studio for a magazine feature. 'I love my Blade to bits,' he said, 'and the 'Blade day was simply superb for rubbing shoulders with others who feel the same way. Getting the chance to ride such a great sportsbike around a fantastic circuit was just the icing on the cake.'

The man himself – Tadao Baba – was there, enjoying the fruits of his success. Big Japanese multi-national companies do not normally single out one individual for success, but such is the presence and character of this man and machine, that Honda has realised that both Baba and the FireBlade are a phenomenon. Baba himself enjoyed meeting owners,

FireBlades as far as the eye can see - Silverstone, 27 June 2000 – the greatest number of CBR900RRs ever assembled in one place came from around the world to attend the inaugural FireBlade day. (Double Red)

getting feedback on models old and current. As he has listened to owners in the past so he will be storing all the knowledge for future models. Baba was surprised – but delighted – to find many owners wanted him to autograph their machines.

One owner of a mint condition K-reg 1992 original with only 4,500 miles on the clock even went one better by getting one side of the cast frame section signed by Baba and the other by one of the test riders involved in the project from the start - Honda UK's Dave Hancock.

At the end of the day, Honda staff managed to shepherd more than 200 FireBlades together on to the start-finish straight to complete a picture of the biggest collection of CBR900RRs ever put together in one place. Can you count them all?

One thing many owners felt, was that the 'Blade truly has character. Many said that they doubted that people would be getting together at a racetrack somewhere in the best part of a decade's time to remember something as unimaginitively titled as an R1…

Riding impressions of the Y2K 'Blade

The year of 2000 'Blade is the son of its father. But it is very different.

Gone is that feeling of brutishness the original gave when you threw a leg over it. It is still a bike which 'feels' big, yes, but the huge, wide tank of old has been replaced by one with much slimmer lines. The riding position is on the comfortable side of sporty – even more so than the R1 - which for 2000, also relaxed its riding position a little. But, point it at a corner and the old 'Blade reminiscences come flooding back.

The steering geometry of 25° and 95mm of rake and trail give it astounding turn in capability. More so than the original – which itself was renowned as a bike which could turn into a corner quicker than much smaller machines. On the race track this handling and better overall feeling from the suspension leaves many believing that between this and an R1, the 'Blade is the easiest to turn into a race machine.

It does have deficiencies compared with the R1, though. As it gives away around 70cc, it lacks the R1's breathtaking torque curve. Below 6,000 revs there is little to write home about, but then at 8,000 revs the thing fair takes off towards the horizon. Early 2000 press 'Blades suffered from differing power outputs – just as the original CBR had done eight years previously. *Bike* magazine found their long-termer producing just 117 EC-corrected bhp at the rear wheel when they received the bike, then – 2,000 miles later – it was pumping out a much healthier 126bhp.

But, it is the best 'Blade yet, by far and judging by the number of new machines at the Honda FireBlade day, there is life in the old dog yet… Also, the 2000 'Blade won *Superbike* magazine's 'Sportsbike of the Year' award.

of the swingarm by 20mm (0.79in) while maintaining the same wheelbase for more progressive rear suspension operation and reduced strain on the 'Blade's drive chain.

The swingarm's suspension system also received carefully calculated revisions in order to provide a wider range of adjustment and compatibility with various rider sizes and riding styles.

Wheels, brakes and tyres

The FireBlade's rolling gear also came in for a reappraisal and upgrade. Its slick, modern-looking cast aluminium triple-spoke wheels replace the previous model's five-spokers, and a new 17-inch front rim replaces the 16-inch wheel used on the FireBlade since its debut in 1992. Finally – it seems – Honda has admitted that the 17-incher, along with its associated wider selection of tyres, is the way to go.

Attached to the huge, muscular rear swingarm is a monstrous 190-rear-section tyre, which will grab as much attention as it does tarmac.

Braking up front is handled by a pair of four-piston calipers gripping bigger, dinner plate-sized 330mm rotors between high-performance sintered metal pads. The rear wheel is stopped by the same 220mm single-piston caliper disc brake used on the 1998-9 model.

And the future?

For Baba-san, the man who has spent a decade honing the FireBlade in the forge of Honda Research and Development, this latest model is the logical progression and most certainly the fruit of the original machine's muscular loins.

Perhaps like design icons such as the Porsche 911, the Mini, and the Volkswagen Beetle, the Honda CBR900RR FireBlade could well outlive its creator, in one form or another.

'Oh, yes,' says Baba, taking another puff on his cigarette. 'I see the FireBlade like my son! I have been to many countries with it and had the opportunity to talk to many people. It is definitely a part of my life. If only I could speak English and German more fluently, it would be even more fascinating to talk to people about the experiences that they have had with the machine. Motorcycling is a universal language. That's what I've found. The age and nationality of

Baba-san's latest in action. (Honda)

the rider don't matter. An exciting bike is an exciting bike the world over. Europe has been the centre of motorcycle culture and it's been here that our Japanese CBR900RR FireBlade was accepted warmly and for that I am so very happy.'

Baba-san may be heading towards his sixties, but a man who still pops to the test track in his leathers to scare the young test riders silly has no intention of ending his involvement with the FireBlade.

'There are many things I still want to do with the bike,' he admits. 'My dreams for the 'Blade will never end! In fact, I really think there will be no end. In 50 years' time, I hope the 'Blade will still be in the process of development. It is just sad that I won't be here on the Earth with it by then.'

If he lives to be 100 years old – no doubt still badgering test riders and engineers on and off the track – Baba-san can rest easy, knowing that in the Honda CBR900RR FireBlade he's built more than just a great bike. He's left behind a motorcycling icon and an enduring legacy for others to follow.

Tadao Baba – would sportsbikes be as advanced as they are today without this man? (Yuko Sugeta)

Technical appendix

1992/3 Honda CBR900RR FireBlade

ENGINE/GEARBOX
Type: liquid-cooled, 16-valve inline four
Capacity: 893cc
Bore x stroke: 70 x 58mm
Compression ratio: 11:1
Carburation: 4 x 38mm Keihin CV
Power
   Claimed: 122bhp @ 10,500rpm
   Tested: 106–114bhp
Torque: 65lb/ft (7.34Nm) @ 8,500rpm
Gearbox: 6-speed
Electrics: 12V/8A battery; 2 x 60/55W headlight

CYCLE PARTS
Chassis: extruded aluminium twin-spar frame,
   box section aluminium swingarm
Suspension
   Front: 45mm telescopic fork, pre-load and
   rebound adjustable
   Rear: Pro-link single shock, seven-way
   preload with compression and rebound
   damping adjustable
Brakes
   Front: 2 x 296mm discs with opposed four
   piston calipers
   Rear: 220mm disc, single piston

TYRES
Bridgestone Battlax radials
   Front: 130/70 ZR16
   Rear: 180/55 ZR18

DIMENSIONS
Wheelbase: 1,405mm (55.3in)
Rake/trail: 24°/90mm (3.5in)
Dry weight: 185kg (407lb)
Seat height: 800mm (31.5in)
Fuel capacity: 18l (4gal)

PERFORMANCE
Top speed: 166.6mph (268.1kph)
Standing quarter mile: 10.54sec/137.7mph
   (221.6kph)
Average miles per gallon: 36mpg (7.8l/100km)

1994/5 Honda CBR900RR FireBlade (1995/6 in USA)

ENGINE/GEARBOX
Type: liquid-cooled, 16-valve inline four
Capacity: 893cc
Bore x stroke: 70 x 58mm
Compression ratio: 11:1
Carburation: 4 x 38mm Keihin CV carbs
Power claimed: 122bhp @ 10,500rpm
Torque: 65lb/ft (7.34Nm) @ 8,500 rpm
Gearbox: 6-speed
Electrics: 12V/8Ah battery; 2 x 60/55W headlights

CYCLE PARTS

Chassis: extruded aluminium twin-spar frame,
  box section aluminium swingarm
Suspension
  Front: 45mm telescopic forks, preload,
  compression and rebound damping adjustable
  Rear: Pro Link rising-rate single shock with
  preload, compression and rebound damping
  adjustable
Brakes
  Front: 2 x 296mm discs, opposed four piston
  calipers
  Rear: 220mm disc, single piston caliper

TYRES

Bridgestone Battlax radials
  Front: 130/70 ZR16
  Rear: 180/55 ZR17

DIMENSIONS

Wheelbase: 1,405mm (55.3in)

Rake/trail: 24°/90mm (3.5in)
Dry weight: 185kg (408lb)
Seat height: 800mm (31.5in)
Fuel capacity: 18l (4gal)

PERFORMANCE

Top speed: 166.2mph (267.4kph) (as tested)
Standing quarter mile: 11.06sec/126.9mph
  (204.2kph)
Average miles per gallon: 38mpg (7.4l/100km)

1996/7 Honda CBR900RR FireBlade

ENGINE/GEARBOX

Type: liquid-cooled, 16-valve inline four
Capacity: 918.5cc
Bore x stroke: 71 x 58mm
Compression ratio: 11.1:1
Carburation: 4 x 38mm Keihin CV carbs
Power claimed: 126bhp @ 10,500rpm

Torque: 67lb/ft (7.57Nm) @ 8,750 rpm
Gearbox: 6-speed
Electrics: 12V/8Ah battery; 2 x 60/55W
  headlights

CYCLE PARTS

Chassis: extruded aluminium twin-spar frame,
  box section aluminium swingarm
Suspension
  Front: 45mm telescopic forks, preload,
  compression and rebound damping
  adjustable
  Rear: Pro-Link rising-rate single shock,
  preload, compression and rebound damping
  adjustable
Brakes
  Front: 2 x 296mm discs, opposed four piston
  calipers
  Rear: 220mm disc, single piston caliper

TYRES

Bridgestone Battlax radials
  Front: 130/70 ZR16
  Rear: 180/55 ZR17

DIMENSIONS

Wheelbase: 1,405mm (55.3in)
Rake/trail: 24°/90mm (3.5in)
Dry weight: 183kg (404lb)
Seat height: 810mm (31.8in)
Fuel capacity: 18l (4.0gal)

PERFORMANCE

Top speed: 167.5mph (269.5kph) (as tested)
Standing quarter mile: 10.7sec/128mph
  (205.9kph)
Average miles per gallon: 38mpg (7.4l/100km)

1998/9 Honda CBR900RR FireBlade

ENGINE/GEARBOX

Type: liquid-cooled, 16-valve inline four
Capacity: 918cc
Bore x stroke: 71mm x 58mm
Compression ratio: 11.1:1
Carburation: 4 x 38mm Keihin CV
  carbs
Power
  Claimed: 128bhp @
  10,500rpm
  Tested: 122bhp.
Torque: 68ft/lb (7.68Nm) @
  8,200 rpm
Gearbox: 6-speed
Electrics: 12V/8Ah battery;
  2 x 60/55W headlights

CYCLE PARTS

Chassis: extruded aluminium twin-
  spar frame, box section
  aluminium swingarm
Suspension
  Front: 45mm telescopic forks, preload,
  compression and rebound damping
  adjustable
  Rear: Pro Link rising-rate single shock,
  preload, compression and rebound damping
  adjustable
Brakes
  Front: 2 x 296mm discs, opposed four piston
  calipers
  Rear: 220mm disc, single piston caliper

TYRES

Bridgestone Battlax radials
  Front: 130/70 ZR16
  Rear: 180/55 ZR17

DIMENSIONS

Wheelbase: 1,405mm (55.3in)

Rake/trail: 24°/95mm (3.7in)
Dry weight: 180kg (396.9lb)
Seat height: 810mm (31.8in)
Fuel capacity: 18l (4.0gal)

PERFORMANCE
Top speed: 167mph (268.7kph) (as tested)
Standing quarter mile: 10.6sec/136mph
  (218.8kph)
Average miles per gallon: 40mpg (7.1l/100km)

2000 Honda FireBlade

ENGINE/GEARBOX
Type: liquid-cooled, 16-valve inline four
Capacity: 929cc
Bore x stroke: 74 x 54mm

Compression ratio: 11.3:1
Carburation: Electronic PGM-FI fuel injection
Power claimed at crank: 151bhp @ 11,000rpm
Torque: 75.95lb/ft (8.68Nm) @ 8,500 rpm
Gearbox: 6-speed
Electrics: 12V/8Ah battery; 3 x H7 Halogen
  headlights

CYCLE PARTS
Chassis: extruded aluminium twin-spar semi-
  pivotless frame, box section aluminium
  swingarm
Suspension
  Front: 43mm inverted HMAS cartridge-type
  telescopic fork with stepless pre-load,
  compression and rebound adjustable
  Rear: Rear Pro-Link with gas-charged HMAS

damper featuring 13-step pre load and
stepless compression and rebound damping
adjustable
Brakes
Front: 2 x 330mm discs, opposed four piston
calipers
Rear: 220mm disc, single piston caliper

TYRES
Front: 120/70 ZR17
Rear: 190/50 ZR17

DIMENSIONS
Wheelbase: 1,400mm (55.1in)
Rake/trail: not available
Dry weight: 170kg (374.85lb)
Seat height: 815mm (32.9in)
Fuel capacity: 18l (4.0gal)

PERFORMANCE
Top speed: 175mph (281.6kph) (estimated)
Standing quarter mile: 10.3sec/133mph
(214kph) (estimated)
Average miles per gallon: 40mpg (7.1l/100km)
(estimated)

Honda FireBlade and its rivals: a technical comparison 1992–4

HONDA CBR900RR FIREBLADE 1992
Engine: liquid-cooled 16-valve inline four
Capacity: 893cc
Power: 113bhp @ 9,500rpm
Torque: 65.1ft/lb (7.36Nm) @ 8,500rpm
Chassis: extruded aluminium twin-spar with
box section swingarm
Suspension
Front: 45mm telescopic forks, pre-load and
rebound damping adjustable
Rear: Pro-Link rising-rate monoshock, pre-
load, rebound and compression adjustable

Brakes
Front: 2 x 296mm discs four-piston opposed
calipers
Rear: 220mm disc single piston caliper
Tyres: Bridgestone Battlax
Front: 130/70 ZR16
Rear: 180/55 ZR17
Wheelbase: 1,405mm (55.3in)
Dry weight: 185kg (407lb)
Top speed: 166.7mph (268.2kph)

YAMAHA FZR1000RU EXUP
Engine: liquid-cooled 20-valve inline
four
Capacity: 1,003cc
Power: 120bhp @ 10,000rpm
Torque: 66.2ft/lb (7.48Nm) @
8,500rpm
Chassis: aluminium Deltabox twin beam
frame
Suspension
Front: 41mm inverted telescopic forks,
pre-load adjustable
Rear: rising-rate monoshock, pre-load and
rebound adjustable
Brakes
Front: 2 x 320mm discs with four piston
opposed calipers
Rear: 267mm disc with single opposed
piston caliper
Tyres: Dunlop Sportmax
Front: 130/60 ZR17
Rear: 170/60 ZR17
Wheelbase: 1,470mm (57.9in)
Dry weight: 214kg (471.9lb)
Top speed: 167mph (268.7kph)

SUZUKI GSX-R1100 1992
Engine: oil-cooled 16-valve inline four
Capacity: 1,127cc
Power: 132bhp @ 9,500rpm
Torque: 83.2ft/lb (9.4Nm) @ 7,500rpm
Chassis: aluminium box-section double cradle

frame, with box-section swingarm
Suspension
   Front: 41mm inverted forks, pre-load,
   rebound and compression adjustable
   Rear: Full-Floater rising-rate monoshock, pre-
   load, rebound and compression damping
   adjustable
Brakes
   Front: 2 x 310mm floating discs with four-
   piston opposed calipers
   Rear: 230mm twin-piston caliper
Tyres: Metzler
   Front: 120/70 ZR17
   Rear: 180/55 ZR17
Wheelbase: 1,535mm (60.4in)
Dry weight: 251kg (553lb)
Top speed: 168mph (270.3kph)

Honda FireBlade and its rivals: a technical comparison 1994–7

HONDA CBR900RR FIREBLADE 1994

Engine: liquid-cooled, 16-valve inline four
Capacity: 893cc
Power claimed: 122bhp @ 10,500rpm
Torque: 65ft/lb (7.35Nm) @ 8,500 rpm
Chassis: extruded aluminium twin-spar frame,
   box section aluminium swingarm
Suspension
   Front: 45mm telescopic forks, preload,
   compression and rebound damping
   adjustable
   Rear: Pro Link rising-rate single shock,
   preload, compression and rebound damping
   adjustable

Brakes
  Front: 2 x 296mm discs, opposed four piston
  calipers
  Rear: 220mm disc, single piston caliper
Tyres: Bridgestone Battlax radials
  Front: 130/70 ZR16
  Rear: 180/55 ZR17
Wheelbase: 1,405mm (55.3in)
Dry weight: 185kg (408lb)
Top speed: 166.2mph (267.4kph)

KAWASAKI ZX-9R B1 NINJA 1994

Engine: liquid-cooled 16-valve inline four
Capacity: 899cc
Power: 125bhp @ 10,500rpm, 137bhp
  unrestricted
Torque: 68ft/lb (7.68Nm) @ 8,500rpm
Chassis: pressed aluminium beam perimeter
  frame, box section aluminium swingarm
Suspension
  Front: 41mm inverted telescopic forks,
  preload, compression and rebound damping
  adjustable
  Rear: Uni-Trak rising-rate single shock,
  preload, compression and rebound damping
  adjustable
Brakes
  Front: 2 x 320mm semi-floating discs with
  opposed four-piston calipers (changed to six
  pistons on the B3 model)
  Rear: 230mm disc, single piston caliper
Tyres: Bridgestone Battlax
  Front: 120/70 ZR17
  Rear: 180/55 ZR17
Wheelbase: 1,440mm (56.7in)
Dry weight: 215kg (474lb)
Top speed: 170mph (273.5kph)

YAMAHA YZF750R 1994

Engine: liquid-cooled 20 valve inline four
Capacity: 749cc
Power claimed: 124bhp @ 12,000rpm
Torque: 60ft/lb (6.78Nm) @ 9,500rpm

Chassis: aluminium Deltabox, box section
  aluminium swingarm
Suspension
  Front: 41mm inverted telescopic fork, preload
  adjustable
  Rear: monocross single shock, preload and
  rebound damping adjustable
Brakes
  Front: 2 x 320mm discs opposed four
  piston calipers
  Rear: 245mm disc opposed piston
  caliper
Tyres: Dunlop Sports Radial
  Front: 120/70 ZR17
  Rear: 180/55 ZR17
Wheelbase: 1,420mm (55.9in)
Dry weight: 195kg (429lb)
Top speed: 154.1mph (247.9kph)

KAWASAKI ZXR750L1 1994

Engine: liquid-cooled 16-valve inline
  four
Capacity: 749cc
Power claimed: 121bhp @ 11,000rpm
Torque: 58ft/lb (6.55Nm) @ 10,000rpm
Chassis: extruded aluminium twin-spar, box
  section aluminium swingarm
Suspension
  Front: 41mm inverted telescopic forks,
  preload and rebound damping adjustable
  Rear: Uni-Trak single shock, preload, ride-
  height and rebound adjustable
Brakes
  Front: 2 x 320mm discs, opposed four piston
  calipers
  Rear: 230mm opposed piston caliper
Tyres: Dunlop Sportmax
  Front: 120/70 ZR17
  Rear: 180/55 ZR17
Wheelbase: 1,430mm (56.3in)
Dry weight: 205kg (451lb)
Top speed: 160mph (257.4kph)

DUCATI 916 1994
Engine: liquid-cooled 8 valve 90 degree V-twin
Capacity: 916cc
Power claimed: 112bhp @ 9,000rpm
Torque: 61ft/lb (6.89Nm) @ 7,500rpm
Chassis: steel trellis
Suspension
   Front: 43mm Showa inverted telescopic
   forks, compression and rebound adjustable
   Rear: Showa compression, preload and
   rebound adjustable
Brakes
   Front: 2 x 320mm Brembo floating discs four
   piston opposed calipers
   Rear: 220mm disc opposed caliper
Tyres: Pirelli Dragon
   Front: 120/70 ZR17
   Rear: 190/50 ZR17
Wheelbase: 1,410mm (55in)
Dry weight: 195kg (429.9lb)

Top speed: 162mph (260.7kph)

HONDA CBR900RR FIREBLADE 1996
Engine: liquid-cooled 16-valve inline four
Capacity: 918cc
Power claimed: 126bhp @ 10,500rpm
Torque: 67ft/lb (7.57Nm) @ 8,750rpm
Chassis: extruded aluminium twin-spar frame,
   box section aluminium swingarm
Suspension
   Front: 45mm telescopic forks, rebound,
   compression and preload adjustable
   Rear: Pro-link, preload, compression and
   rebound adjustable
Brakes
   Front: 2 x 296mm discs with opposed four
   piston calipers
   Rear: 220mm disc single piston caliper
Tyres: Bridgestone Battlax
   Front: 130/70 ZR16

Rear: 180/55 ZR17
Wheelbase: 1,405mm (55.3in)
Dry weight: 183kg (403.5lb)
Top speed: 167mph (268.7kph)

Suzuki GSX-R750 1996

Engine: liquid-cooled 16-valve inline four
Capacity: 749cc
Power claimed: 126bhp @ 12,000rpm
Torque: 59ft/lb (6.67Nm) @10,000rpm
Chassis: extruded aluminium twin-spar frame,
    box section aluminium swingarm
Suspension
    Front: 43mm inverted telescopic forks, pre-
    load, compression and rebound adjustable
    Rear: rising-rate monoshock
Brakes
    Front: 2 x 320mm discs six-piston opposed
    calipers
    Rear: 220mm disc opposed caliper
Tyres: Michelin Hi-Sports
    Front: 120/70 ZR17
    Rear: 190/50 ZR17
Wheelbase: 1,400mm (55.1in)
Dry weight: 179kg (395lb)
Top speed: 164mph (263.9kph)

Yamaha YZF1000 Thunderace 1996

Engine: liquid-cooled 20 valve inline four
Capacity: 1,002cc
Power claimed: 130bhp @ 9,900rpm
Torque: 74ft/lb (8.36Nm) @ 8,400rpm
Chassis: aluminium Deltabox twin-spar
Suspension
    Front: 48mm telescopic forks, pre-load,
    compression and rebound adjustable
    Rear: rising-rate monoshock, pre-load,
    compression and rebound adjustable
Brakes
    Front: 2 x 298mm discs four piston opposed
    calipers
    Rear: 245mm disc two-piston caliper
Tyres: Bridgestone Battlax

Front: 120/70 ZR17
    Rear: 180/55 ZR17
Wheelbase: 1,425mm (55.6in)
Dry weight: 198kg (435.6lb)
Top speed: 168mph (270.3kph)

Kawasaki ZX-7R 1996

Engine: liquid-cooled 16-valve inline four
Capacity: 748cc
Power: 111bhp @ 11,400rpm
Torque: 57.5ft/lb (6.5Nm) @ 9,000rpm
Chassis: extruded aluminium twin-spar
Suspension
    Front: 43mm inverted telescopic forks, pre-
    load, compression and rebound adjustable
    Rear: Uni-Trak rising-rate monoshock, pre-
    load, compression and rebound adjustable
Brakes
    Front: 2 x 320mm discs six piston opposed
    calipers
    Rear: 205mm disc two-piston caliper
Tyres: Dunlop Sportmax
    Front: 120/70 ZR17
    Rear: 190/50 ZR17
Wheelbase: 1,435mm (56in)
Dry weight: 203kg (447lb)
Top speed: 165mph (265.5kph)

Honda FireBlade and its rivals: a technical comparison 1998–9

Honda CBR900RR FireBlade 1998

Engine: liquid-cooled 16-valve inline four
Capacity: 918cc
Power: 122bhp @ 10,200rpm
Torque: 68ft/lb (7.68Nm) @ 8,200rpm
Chassis: extruded aluminium twin-spar with
    box-section swingarm
Suspension
    Front: 45mm telescopic, pre-load,
    compression and rebound adjustable
    Rear: Pro-Link rising-rate monoshock, pre-
    load, compression, rebound adjustable

Brakes
  Front: 2 x 310mm discs four piston opposed
  calipers
  Rear: 220mm disc two piston caliper
Tyres: Bridgestone Battlax
  Front: 130/70 ZR16
  Rear: 180/50 ZR17
Wheelbase: 1,405mm (55.3in)
Dry weight: 180kg (396.9lb)
Top speed: 168mph (270.3kph)

KAWASAKI **ZX-9R C1** NINJA
Engine: liquid-cooled 16-valve inline four
Capacity: 899cc
Power: 130bhp @ 10,000rpm
Torque: 72ft/lb (8.14Nm) @ 9,100rpm
Chassis: extruded aluminium twin-spar with
  box-section swingarm
Suspension
  Front: 46mm telescopic forks, pre-load,
  compression, rebound adjustable
  Rear: Uni-Trak rising-rate monoshock, pre-
  load, compression, rebound adjustable
Brakes
  Front: 2 x 296mm six-piston opposed
  calipers
  Rear: 220mm disc two piston caliper
Tyres: Bridgestone Battlax

Front: 120/70 ZR17
Rear: 180/55 ZR17
Wheelbase: 1,415mm (55.2in)
Dry weight: 183kg (403.5lb)
Top speed: 170mph (273.5kph)

YAMAHA **YZF-R1**
Engine: liquid-cooled 20 valve inline four
Capacity: 998cc
Power: 138bhp @ 9,800rpm
Torque: 79ft/lb (8.93Nm) @ 8,800rpm
Chassis: extruded aluminium Deltabox, box-
  section swingarm
Suspension
  Front: 41mm inverted telescopic forks, pre-
  load, compression and rebound adjustable
  Rear: rising-rate monoshock, pre-load,
  compression and rebound adjustable
Brakes
  Front: 2 x 298mm discs with four piston
  opposed calipers
  Rear: 245mm disc with two piston caliper
Tyres: Metzler MEZ3
  Front: 120/70 ZR17
  Rear: 190/50 ZR17
Wheelbase: 1,395mm (54.4in)
Dry weight: 177kg (390.3lb)
Top speed: 173mph (278.4kph)

Index